BULL$EYE

Foreword by Bob Proctor, of *The Secret*

ROBERT KENNEDY

ROBERT KENNEDY PUBLISHING

Copyright ©2012
Robert Kennedy Publishing Inc.
400 Matheson Blvd. West
Mississauga, ON L5R 3M1
Canada

Library and Archives Canada Cataloguing
in Publication

Kennedy, Robert, 1938-
    Bull's eye : targeting your life for real financial
    wealth and personal fulfillment /
    Robert Kennedy.

Includes index.
ISBN 978-1-55210-100-1

1. Success. 2. Self-actualization (Psychology).
I. Title.

BF637.S8K46 2012   158.1
C2011-905393-4

Robert Kennedy Publishing
BOOK DEPARTMENT

MANAGING DIRECTOR
Wendy Morley

SENIOR EDITOR
Amy Land

EDITOR, ONLINE AND PRINT
Meredith Barrett

ASSOCIATE EDITOR
Rachel Corradetti

ONLINE EDITOR AND
SOCIAL MEDIA COORDINATOR
Kiersten Corradetti

EDITORIAL ASSISTANTS
Brittany Seki, Chelsea Kennedy

ART DIRECTOR
Gabriella Caruso Marques

ASSISTANT ART DIRECTOR
Jessica Pensabene Hearn

EDITORIAL DESIGNER
Brian Ross

ART ASSISTANT
Kelsey-Lynn Corradetti

MARKETING COORDINATOR
Patricia D'Amato

SENIOR WEB DESIGNER
Chris Barnes

10 9 8 7 6 5 4 3 2 1

Distributed in Canada by:
NBN (National Book Network)
67 Mowat Ave., Suite 241
Toronto, ON M6K 3E3

Distributed in U.S.A. by:
NBN (National Book Network)
15200 NBN Way
Blue Ridge Summit, PA
17214 U.S.A.

Printed in Canada

CONTENTS

CONTENTS

FOREWORD

Bob Proctor

Much like the Bible, which is actually 66 books under one cover, *Bull's Eye* is a complete library of information disguised as a single book – and what a valuable book it is. If you are seeking a compilation of what is, in my opinion, some of the best information on success, then *Bull's Eye* should be your bible. It is so well written, so complete. *Bull's Eye* fascinated me, as I'm sure it will you.

For the past 50 years I, too, have studied the foundational principles of a successful life. I have thousands of books in my personal library on the subject. I place *Bull's Eye* right up there with Napoleon Hill's great work *The Law of Success*.

Robert's research and experience are impressive and, by anyone's standard, he would be considered a very successful person. Everyone who knows him well will be quick to tell you that he has spent his entire life gathering and testing the various philosophies, skills and strategies required to create a successful life. Robert is refreshingly candid about his mistakes, which will not only help you avoid making the same ones, but will also benefit you because he has weeded out what doesn't work and documented that which he has proved does work.

Many years ago Napoleon Hill wrote, "No person has a chance to enjoy permanent success until he begins to look in a mirror for the real cause of all his mistakes." *Bull's Eye* will become a mirror for you as it has for me.

As your eyes move from page to page, you will realize that Robert Kennedy has approached the various aspects of successful living much like a master astronomer. He's devised theories, conducted research, collected and analyzed data, charted the planets and reported on how each one affects the others, in turn helping us understand the fundamental nature of the universe.

Bull's Eye has a tremendous beginning. In the first section, Robert opens with a power suggestion: "Choose a High-Payoff Target." After decades of working in the field of personal development, I have found this to be crucial advice. The vast majority of the population doesn't even set goals, and the individuals who do, set them too low. By immersing yourself in this book, you will definitely be leaps and bounds ahead of everyone else.

From the first page of *Bull's Eye* to the very last, Robert's writing will open your mind to new ways of seeing the world. It will cause you to stretch. As you become familiar with his philosophy, you will realize that setting a high-payoff target does not take any more energy than the Chicken Little goals that dominate the minds of the masses, and by working smarter, hitting that target is definitely within your reach. In fact, to paraphrase the front cover of this book, failure is not an option.

I love Robert's approach in the second chapter, "Make Sure You've Got a Good Shot at Success." He wants you to begin with the idea of a big win. Robert sees no value in developing your mind for small wins – and he is right on the mark. Keep in mind Robert Kennedy has rubbed shoulders with some absolute giants in business and industry. His theories are not based on pie-in-the-sky concepts that were dreamed up by him and his buddies over a few beers after a ball game.

In the chapter "Prepare Yourself for a Downturn," Robert helps you anticipate and plan for the obstacles and setbacks that will inevitably come. There's a natural rhythm in life; summer never follows summer. When you get hit with a downturn and you are prepared, you don't even have to slow down – and you never quit. You can keep on keeping on.

In "Scared Money Never Wins," Robert explains how the very word "scared" sets up a negative vibration in your mind. Scared never attracts positive. Keep in mind, energy always attracts like energy. That chapter is followed by one whose title is a suggestion every successful person would surely agree with: "Apply Faith." While reading this book, your faith will continually expand. It will grow as you move from one chapter to the next. You will become more aware of the power you have within.

Throughout *Bull's Eye*, Robert shares several interesting stories that not only add interest and help keep you focused, but also give you an inside look at who Robert Kennedy really is. Some stories will cause you to laugh out loud, and one is quite heartrending. He does such a good job recounting these stories you will feel as if you are right there as he shares them with you.

Robert has also included in-depth interviews with a number of individuals from different professions, all of whom have enjoyed massive success. As you read through the interviews, some common themes will arise and it will become apparent that all of these successful people have followed the principles that Robert has laid out for you in this book.

But, before I give too much away, let me assure you that the further you get into *Bull's Eye*, the more you are going to like it. By following the strategies for applying this powerful information that Robert has laid out, you will develop an expanded awareness that will carry you to achieve any goal you set.

Permit me to suggest that you make the same decision I made 50 years ago after Napoleon Hill's *Think and Grow Rich* was placed in my hands. I decided that I would make Hill's philosophy a part of my way of thinking, a part of my way of life. It was a decision that has rewarded me over and over again. *Bull's Eye* is now in your hands. Keep it close to you and make Robert Kennedy's rich, rewarding philosophy a part of your way of thinking, a part of your way of life.

Bob Proctor
Contributor to *The Secret* and best-selling author of *You Were Born Rich*

INTRODUCTION

Prostitutes, Pedophiles and Adventures in Home Taxidermy: My Unbelievably Ballsy Path to Abundance

"It has come to our attention that you are marketing chicken manure as a hair-growing product. There is no proof of the efficacy of this ingredient. Please therefore terminate your business immediately or face the probability of legal action."

– Excerpt from a cease and desist letter sent to me by the British Trade Association in the 1960s

Yes, it may seem surprising that someone who owns a multimillion-dollar health and fitness publishing company would start out his guide to success with an anecdote about his short-lived hair-growth venture, but as the title of this section states, sometimes I can be a little ballsy. And a little stupid. That's why I want to begin by telling you a few things about myself; then you can fully realize what an idiot I was during my earlier years on the planet. Kind of an "if I can do it so can you" type of thing, but also a way of helping you learn from my mistakes. As sportscaster Al Bernstein says, "Success is often the result of taking a misstep in the right direction."

So, back to the chicken manure. It was the 1960s and Britain's biggest newspaper ran a story on several chicken farm workers in the north of England whose job it was to shovel the stuff. In the course of the day they would get it on their hands, and then wipe the sweat from their heads. They swore that this repeated action had caused hair to grow on their balding pates. I know, I know. Just writing this stuff makes me wonder about my sanity, but it is true. Remember I was quite young.

Long story short, I visited a local chicken farm and asked if I could buy a sack of chicken poop. The farmer was delighted, if somewhat confused, and gave me a sackful, gratis. I then bought myself some small containers and arranged with one of my schoolteacher colleagues (I was teaching art at Tottenham Technical College at the time) to have the main ingredient pasteurized and mixed with petroleum jelly. A simple label and I was in the mail-order business. My small classified ad read: "Balding? Try our pasteurized chicken-poop remedy. Results guaranteed or full money refund. Just £1."

Well, I never dreamed there were so many balding men (and more than a few women) in the UK. I was inundated with orders – mailbags full. And amazingly I had to make only two refunds. Even more incredible were the letters of satisfaction and claims for repeat orders "because the stuff works." One man claimed that he even started to grow hair on his hands!

The money poured in and although the markup was low I was making a profit. Until, that is, I received the above-mentioned cease and desist letter from the British Trade Commission. Oops!

I cancelled the classified ads that had been running in *Health & Strength* magazine (and others) and presto! I was out of the hair-growth business. A few weeks later, my art school friend Gino came to visit me at my small London apartment. I told him the bizarre story. He raised an eyebrow in disbelief. "Well, what happened to the rest of the chicken shit then?" he challenged.

I thought for a moment, and then remembered where I had left it. We hurried over to the outdoor cellar used for storing coal. As I opened the bag with great trepidation, a huge collection of large bluebottle flies swarmed out from the sack, hitting both Gino and me in the face and filling the room with their buzzing presence. Gino fell on the floor in laughter, tears streaming from his eyes.

"Now do you believe me?" I said.

He looked up from the floor, still laughing. "Yup!" he said. "I think you've made your point."

I'd be lying, though, if I tried to act like the first ballsy-slash-stupid thing I've done was the chicken-poop scheme. When I was a kid I couldn't apply myself to my schoolwork and my grades showed it. I wasn't the worst in my class of 34, but I wasn't far from it. My parents were not happy. I was far too casual about things.

One time I forgot to take my books home and was unable to do my math homework. The next morning at school, a classmate let me hurriedly copy out one of his math assignments. Unfortunately, his arithmetic was incorrect and Mr. Nicholson, the math teacher, noticed the similarity of the math. He took me to his study and thrashed me with "grandpa," his most feared cane. I was 11 years old and had never had a beating like that. I swear during that brutal caning my heart stopped. I knew I had done wrong in copying someone else's work, but never in a million years did I deserve that unbelievably severe punishment. I fell to the floor screaming in pain, pleading for him to stop. He shouted and forced me to my feet to continue the beating until I totally collapsed.

At home a couple of days later, my mother saw my bare behind and gasped in shock. "What on earth happened to you?" she screamed. I didn't know what she was talking about. When I looked in the mirror I could see the whole of my backside was black and purple with deep parallel welts running from side to side. I had to explain the circumstances, which up until then I had kept to myself.

Three weeks later my parents had to go on a three-day trip and arranged to have me boarded for that period at the school. While I was taking a bath, Mr. Nicholson sidled up to the side and took the bar of soap out of my hand. "Make sure you clean behind your ears, Kennedy," he said with a cynical smile. Then the slippery soap popped out of his hand into the bathwater. Immediately his chubby hands were in the water, searching for the soap. Even at 11 years of age I understood exactly what he was up to and covered my genital area with my hands.

Not long after that, two 15-year-old boys in the school were caught having sex in an upper area of the ancient school building known as the belfry. They were immediately expelled, but before they left, spilled the beans on who had taught and encouraged them in their actions: Mr. Nicholson. It soon emerged that his predilections had long involved children. He was shipped off to Australia with no legal proceedings or charges whatsoever. Today he would have been charged and sent to jail.

At school, as I got into my teens, I started to show an interest in writing, to such an extent that I regularly received

A's for my essays. Art was also a subject that saw me at the top of the class, and because of this latter ability my mother suggested that I follow through with further education in art.

Attending Norwich Art School was one of the most exciting times of my life. I had to travel an hour by train every day from Thetford to Norwich and then walk a mile to St. George's Street where the art school was situated. I loved it.

I remember my very first life-drawing class when Jenny, the subject we were directed to sketch, emerged from a dressing room, stood in the middle of the circle of easels and eager eyes and promptly dropped her robe. Our giggles and snickers were extremely hard to contain in the otherwise serious atmosphere.

Life drawing was a three-times-a-week event. What was originally a novel adventure soon became a mundane chore that was to become our least favorite class, taking position behind stone carving, oil painting and ceramics. Whether or not I was naturally ambitious I don't know, but unlike many artistic types, I had definitely developed a money consciousness by the age of 17. As soon as I had learned to paint with a modicum of proficiency, I would take my paints and canvas out to the countryside, plop myself down adjacent to an expensive-looking home and start to paint. In virtually every case, the owner of the house would eventually come traipsing out to see what I was doing.

"I just had to paint your beautiful home," I would say. "It's so well situated and elegantly built. I love the shape of the windows." Not once did the owner pass up the opportunity to ask about buying my painting, and in almost every case a sale was made. I would ask for £1 (about $2), but by today's standards I guess that would translate to about $15. Cheap, of course, but I was a mere student and I wanted to make a sale. To ask for more would have definitely given me fewer sales – and what would I have done with a bunch of unsold oil paintings of other people's houses?

Even though I loved art school, my real passion was coarse fishing. When I was seven my father, home from fighting the Germans with the British army in World War II, had taken me to the local River Thet, and we caught dace. It was thrilling for me to be with my Dad, whom I had hardly seen during the war, and even more thrilling to be taught how to fish. Dace are a fast-water fish and, along with roach, chub, bream, carp, rudd, pike and perch, are designated as coarse fish. Game fishing (trout and salmon) was for the upper class of Brit, the rich who could afford the excessive fees to access the game-fishing waters. The British Isles and nearby countries like Holland and Belgium have literally millions of coarse fishing enthusiasts. Like me, many people were fanatical about one day catching a record-breaking carp or perch. Coarse fishermen would genuinely prefer to catch a two-pound roach than a 30-pound salmon.

While in art school, and because of my interest in angling, I decided out of the blue to write an article about pike fishing for a new English magazine titled *Angling Times.* A month later I was shocked to get a check in the mail for £5 ($10), with a letter from the editor thanking me for my submission. My article appeared the following month and I was so thrilled I bought three copies.

I just couldn't believe that a magazine would pay for something I wrote. Talk about a high. I had new confidence in myself. Now I was a writer and, boy, was I going to make the most of it. I wrote for every fishing magazine in the UK.

At one time an editor asked if I could supply photographs to go along with my articles. I bought a used and somewhat battered 35 mm Pentax that very day. In order to get an exciting photo for the article I had written, I actually bought a fish from the Chelsea fishmonger and took a subway train with my fishing rod, camera and tripod to disembark at Richmond-on-Thames.

I promptly concocted a scene with me holding a fishing rod and, with any luck, the fish appearing to be breaking the surface with an almighty splash. With my Pentax attached to the tripod, angled and focused just right, I would attach the fish to my line, set the eight-second self-timer on the camera, and after counting to six I would throw the fish up in the air and grab the rod as though I were making the catch of a lifetime. I took an entire roll of 24 images, hoping that at least one of the photographs would be believable.

When I got to my homemade darkroom to develop the film my heart sank, as most of the images showed the fish six feet above the water. But then, miracle of miracles, on the very last frame there it was ... me wearing my fisherman's hat, leaning back, the rod bowed, line taut and the underbelly of the fish clearly visible as it caused an impressive splash, turning my visualized plan into reality in the pages of the *Angling Times*. It was exciting to make a little extra money here and there, and my ambition was in high gear all the time.

My next adventure was taxidermy. The point of angling for coarse fish in the UK was to catch fish that were extra large or even record-breaking for their species. Typically a two-pound roach, a five-pound chub, an eight-pound bream, a four-pound perch and a 20-pound pike would all be considered "specimen" weight catches. When we were lucky or clever enough to catch one of these, we either photographed it and returned it to the water alive or kept it and stuffed it.

But taxidermy was expensive, so with my mind forever on the possibilities of making money, I devised a plan to come up with a home taxidermy course. My first step was to get a professional taxidermist to let me sit in on the procedure of actually stuffing and mounting a fish. Someone in the area had landed a 27-pound pike and was willing to pay for it to be stuffed. I was lucky to be able to observe the process. I wrote out the procedure step by step and had it printed up in a booklet. Small ads in the various angling newspapers brought me a small but regular profit.

My next step was to pay for a booth space at Britain's annual Angling Expo in London to sell my Home Taxidermy Courses. Sales were brisk and ultimately attracted the BBC, who asked if they could film a live demonstration of how to stuff a fish. They agreed to come back the next day with their TV cameras.

The next day arrived, but I had no fish with which to demonstrate. I roamed the other booths at the expo and, as luck would have it, one of the exhibitors had three large, live perch in a tank and had arrived in the morning to find that they had not survived because their aeration feed was cut off overnight by the expo organizers anxious to save on hydro. The perch-owning exhibitor was delighted that I was willing to take the dead fish off his hands. I was in business.

My demonstration was ready to go and the BBC live cameras were rolling. I talked rather eloquently about the procedure, if I do say so myself. However, having never stuffed a perch before, I was unaware of the toughness of the skin. I pushed, pressed and stabbed to break through that perch skin to no avail. With cameras rolling and sweat streaming from my temples, I finally managed to get the point through but couldn't continue the horizontal cut. Fortunately, I had brought a pair of scissors, which proved to be my face-saver. I inserted them into the opening and with all the power I could muster, cut through that perch hide for the full nine inches. From then on the demo was a cinch.

Later, when the cameras had disappeared, I noticed blood on my right hand. I had created an open sore and drawn blood from the monumental effort I had put into the making of that nine-inch cut. The pain was nothing to the humiliation I was subjected to by a bunch of purist anglers who openly berated me for the "unnecessary killing of those beautiful perch." They were so vociferous that a small crowd gathered and joined in on the attack. I tried in vain to explain that the fish were not mine, and that they had died overnight at someone else's booth. But the anger had created so much noise that my words were neither heard nor understood. That night, I placed a classified ad in *Angling Times:* "Home Taxidermy Course business for sale, £200 or best offer." A mini-bidding war was created and I ended up selling for £310 ($600). I considered this a grand success at the time.

Let's see now. Just what was the stupidest thing I've ever done?

Here it is: While I was attending Norwich Art School in the '50s I developed a fascination – no, a love – for the paintings of Henri de Toulouse-Lautrec. You are likely familiar with his work if not his name. He was born into French aristocracy, but failed to grow in height after the age of 10 or so. He was famous for his oil paintings of Parisian nightlife, many of which involved images of pimps and prostitutes painted during his frequent visits to brothels in Paris' Montmartre district.

Well, at 18 years of age I decided I wanted to be like Monsieur Toulouse-Lautrec. I was convinced that the increased quality and realism of my work would bring me a higher price for my paintings. So, one Saturday I trundled a canvas, my oil paints and brushes off to London's Soho in search of a brothel, the likes of which I had never seen before. Finding one was far easier than I thought. A scantily clad young lady, with tousled hair draped around her overly made-up face and a skirt a good 15 inches above her knees, beckoned me through a doorway lit up by a single red bulb.

I descended the dark stairs to reach a large, even darker room. As my eyes adjusted to the lack of light I became aware of 12 to 15 women sitting around on couches and reclining seats. "Prostitutes," I thought to myself, slightly awestruck, "they're all prostitutes." Without a second thought I got busy with my canvas and paints; at last I was mimicking my hero, painting the low life in a real honest-to-goodness brothel. I hadn't even asked permission and, truth be told, when the women realized I was there to make art and not to buy their services, they warmed up to me and showed great interest in my painting as it developed.

After a couple of hours two uniformed policemen came onto the scene. One sneered at the girls. "Business a little lean tonight, scumbags?"

The women said nothing. The second cop followed up with "Yeah, who'd want to pay good money for these sluts anyway?"

And now here is where I got unbelievably ballsy and incredibly stupid.

Maybe I was feeling sorry for the women. Or maybe I was feeling chivalrous. Whatever the reason, I raised my hand as though to sweep the first cop to the side. "Do you mind, officer," I commanded, "I'm trying to paint these ladies and you're standing in the way!" Well, this brought a collective howl of laughter from the women, who had remained silent up until now. I heard one say, "Wow! He's a cheeky one isn't he?" implying that I must be the bravest man in London.

Well, that was it. The two cops looked at each other, angry that they had been laughed at by a group of prostitutes and openly ridiculed by some 18-year-old kid, and made a beeline for me. Knocking over my paints and stepping on my canvas, they dragged me up the stairs. When they got me out on the street they pushed me up against the wall of the building and handcuffed me. I was then dragged to a nearby paddy wagon and questioned for an hour before they released me, tattered and bruised, to the hustle and bustle of Soho's nightlife. Can you spell insanely stupid? That's me.

In the 1970s, I found a way to incorporate my interest in both physical fitness and writing. I was inspired by the fact that Mr. Charles Atlas had sold in excess of 30 million non-apparatus bodybuilding courses worldwide. Buoyed by the knowledge that he had built his body mainly through training with weights, and that the course had actually been written by an English friend of mine, Dr. Fred Tilney – Atlas himself hadn't written a single word – I decided that I too could write and market a bodybuilding course. I tackled the job and wrote the entire course in just three days with only two hours' sleep each night.

I titled it *Hercules II* and it contained 12 lessons that were mailed out individually each week. Once again I was in the mail-order business with high hopes of making good money. I got myself a post-office box and placed full-page ads in numerous men's magazines. When the ads broke, I rushed to the post office to check my mail. Nothing. I waited another week. Still nothing. I couldn't believe there were zero responses to my ads.

On the third week, I again opened my post office box; still nothing. But wait! There was a small white card lying at the bottom of the post office box that I must have previously missed. It read: "Please present this card at the post office's front desk." When I gave the post office official the card he promptly disappeared, while shouting to three of his colleagues. I began to worry that I was in some kind of trouble.

"Why didn't you bring the card to us earlier?" he asked.
"I didn't see it, sir," I replied, using my most polite voice.
"Well," he said, "you've got yourself a hell of a lot of mail."
I looked at him and his colleagues, each of whom was holding two packed mailbags of what turned out to be paid orders for my new bodybuilding course. *Hercules II*

kept me well fed and watered for the next five years. Even after paying my taxes I had enough to buy my first real home.

As business boomed, I was getting more ambitious, or more stupid. Maybe both. Out of the blue, with no real money in my pocket, it suddenly occurred to me to seek a better life and immigrate to Canada, known to Brits as the land of opportunity.

I had always been an avid reader of bodybuilding magazines and had continued my writing career, after moving to Canada, by writing for various muscle publications, including Joe Weider's *Muscle Power,* John Grimek's *Muscular Development,* Peary Rader's *Iron Man,* Oscar Heidenstam's *Health and Strength* and Dave Prowse's *Power.*

Writing for bodybuilding magazines was more a labor of love. The payment was nominal but I still got a thrill every time I received a letter that ended with, "Please find enclosed your check in payment for your article."

After teaching art for a few years in Canada, I decided to go into business for myself full time. Having an interest in physical fitness and having built a bit of a name for myself, I started an exercise magazine. I had attended numerous bodybuilding and fitness contests both in Europe and in North America. I had become friends with such people as

Mr. Universe Reg Park, Jack LaLanne and a young Austrian by the name of Arnold Schwarzenegger.

With the help of my art school buddy Gino, who by this time had also moved to Canada with his wife and daughter, I produced a body-improvement magazine, which I titled *MuscleMag International.* And here's the real stupid part: With no money and no orders, I persuaded a printer to print up 110,000 copies.

When the magazines arrived I had nowhere to store them. My kitchen, living room and bedroom ended up full of stacks of boxes of them. I scanned the Yellow Pages under "magazine distribution." Nada. Then, by constantly asking around, I found a small office in Niagara Falls run by Capital Distributing. I took a handful of magazines to show and had the fingers of both hands crossed. The owner (I forget his name) flicked through a copy and threw it back at me across his desk. I may not remember his name, but I sure do remember his words.

"You mean to tell me you have 110,000 of these magazines and nowhere to go?"

I swallowed a couple of times. "Yes, sir." I gulped.

He paused, looked me over. "We'll take them!" he replied. My day was made. Now, I really was in the magazine business.

Publishing is a tough business, but somehow I've kept it going through all the ups and downs. Believe it or not, the average sale of a newsstand magazine is 33 percent. So if you distribute 300,000, you sell 100,000 but 200,000 unsold copies, magazines that you paid your printer to create, get destroyed. Incidentally, an amazing newsstand sell-through is 50 percent and this is very seldom achieved.

The magazines I publish cover subjects of health, nutrition and exercise. I like to publish subjects I know and feel passionately about. I have plans to publish a magazine on angling and one on fine art, but I won't do that until I have worked out my target reader in each case.

When you publish magazines, it's not a huge step to publish books. Robert Kennedy Publishing currently publishes about 20 books a year. This is another precarious business. (Aren't they all?) Most books, even those put out by the big publishers, lose money or at best only break even after years on bookshelves in the various outlets.

On the other hand, if you get a winner like my wife's *Eat-Clean Diet*® series, which has sold more than two million copies, then you can make some good money. My wife is Tosca Reno and, boy, am I proud of her. She's amazing on so many levels. A true gem. I never stop thanking my lucky stars that she said yes when I asked for her hand in marriage.

We live in a nice house, formerly owned by Chris Haney, one of the inventors of Trivial Pursuit. We have four children, Chelsea, Kelsey-Lynn, Kiersten and Rachel. My son Braden died in 2011 at the age of 23. Tosca and I work out regularly and eat clean (as you might guess). We don't smoke, and we drink only the occasional glass of wine. Most importantly, we love the work we do. We love life. We still have goals. When people ask me what I do for excitement, I say: "I married it!"

As you're probably beginning to realize, I've always had an inner drive for more. Don't ask me where it came from. Whether it was pure selfishness or uncontrolled greed for a richer life, I can't say. I only know that I was always ambitious. I wanted to help people, true, but I also hoped to travel the world, experience the good life and, I'll freely admit, I wanted abundance, a nice car, a luxury home and cash in the bank.

Before we go any further, I desperately want you to understand that you can start from anywhere and create an abundant life for yourself. It's time to get serious about climbing the mountain of financial success. Let's get down to business. Right now, are you making a bare living, just making ends meet at the end of the month, or worse, not making ends meet at the end of the month? This is because you have fallen into a rut. Whether working for others, for yourself or not working at all, you are in a hole, digging to get out. But you don't need to dig. That just makes the hole deeper. You need a ladder. Your "ladder" has to take the form of new thinking. Consider this book the ladder that will help you get out of your hole. Things have to change. It's time to stop digging and start climbing. Even after all of my mishaps, I was able to do it.

Now it's your turn.

This book and the rest of your life are in your hands.

To get the most out *Bull's Eye*, I want you to:
- Promise yourself you will read this book from beginning to end.
- If you don't understand any part, read it over until you do.
- Have a pen or highlighter and mark off salient points. I have provided the "Aim for the Bull" section at the end of each chapter to help you with this.
- Apply these principles at every opportunity, using this book to keep you on track.
- Take notes and write in the margins and in the "Notes" section at the back of the book.
- As you read, stop frequently and consider how you can apply the principles to design your own success.
- Never doubt that you will be a huge success as your life unfolds.

Choose a
High-Payoff Target

bull's-eye:

> **a:** the center of a target; *also*: something central
> or crucial **b:** a shot that hits the bull's-eye; *broadly*:
> something that precisely attains a desired end
> - *Merriam-Webster's Collegiate Dictionary*

Back in the early '70s I started a magazine devoted to physical culture, and, unlikely as it may seem, one of the subscribers was Jean Paul Getty, the richest man in the world. Because of my position as publisher and our mutual interest in the iron game, Jean Paul and I became friends.

I would frequently visit him for a very civilized tea at Sutton Place, his magnificent 15th-century country home. At this stage of my life I was moderately successful with my own business. I had developed an exercise program which was offered by mail order (no Internet or toll-free order lines in those days), I had a couple of magazines, several stores, a small rental apartment complex and I was publishing a variety of books on nutrition and exercise. However, I was then, as I still am today, eager to learn more, especially from someone of the status of Mr. Jean Paul Getty.

TARGET 1

At one point, Jean Paul was very frustrated with his Italian organization. Unlike most of his other affiliations, the Italian oil company seldom made a profit. When I asked him why, he gave me a guarded answer, not wishing to bore me with minute details. He simply said, "Every business must be run with a sense of thrift. Even when income is high there will be no profit unless expenses are kept in check." Good advice for us all to keep in mind – and a philosophy that would explain why he had a pay phone installed in his

> EVERY BUSINESS MUST BE RUN WITH A SENSE OF THRIFT. EVEN WHEN INCOME IS HIGH THERE WILL BE NO PROFIT UNLESS EXPENSES ARE KEPT IN CHECK.
>
> *– Jean Paul Getty*

house (something the British press were constantly riding him about). In Mr. Getty's defense, though, apparently it was a pastime of visitors, employees and maintenance workers to make costly long-distance calls to people around the world ("Hey! Guess where I'm calling from?"), and it was his estate manager Robina Lund who finally put her foot down and suggested the phone.

On another occasion, I asked Jean Paul, "What more can I do to increase my business?"

To which he replied, "Just come up with something else that works and that has the features customers want, and dream up innovative ways to let people know about that product or service."

You can't get any simpler than that, can you? Give people what they want and you will get all that you want. It's a mantra that has been repeated throughout the ages and

> GIVE PEOPLE WHAT THEY
> WANT AND YOU WILL GET
> ALL THAT YOU WANT.

this advice has served me well. (And, lucky you, it is just one of the many secrets of success I'm ready to share with you in the following pages.) But before you heed Jean Paul Getty's directive of giving people what they want, you first need to find out what *you* want. Yes, decide what you want. And do it as soon as possible. Most people don't get what they want because they haven't decided *what* they want. Sometimes, as illustrated in the following incident, realizing exactly what you *don't* want is a great place to start. In fact, it is what spurred me to take the initial leap that got me to where I am today.

My parents, bless them, were both teachers and wanted me to follow in their footsteps. I conceded and taught for eight years, but I had an inner drive for more.

> ## WRITE DOWN ALL YOUR
> ## WANTS AND NEEDS.

Not that I was unhappy as a teacher. I enjoyed my pupils and the other staff. We had some good times – memories galore. Working with kids is always interesting. Then one day, while I was teaching at Tottenham Technical College in London, a colleague who was head of his department came into the staffroom, beaming from ear to ear. "I've just got myself a new car. Come and see, Kennedy, it's a beauty." I happily followed him out to the college parking lot. We stopped at an old rusted out Ford Capri.

"Isn't she a beaut?" he said. "I'm going to call her Maggie." I actually thought he was joking, and started looking around for a newer vehicle.

TARGET 1

When I realized he was deadly serious I crossed the fingers of both hands behind my back. "Yessir, what a beauty," I said as I forced a fake smile. "Congratulations."

When I got back to my small apartment I had a serious talk with myself. Here I was teaching at college level, no chance of being promoted to head of my art department for at least five years. Even if I was promoted, I could still hope to do no better than my colleague with his rusted-out Ford Capri. Before the end of the week had arrived, I had given in my notice to the principal. I told my devastated parents I wanted more. They were not happy, but I was a man on a mission.

If you, too, want a life full of excitement and abundance I can assure you it is there for the taking. You can succeed. Write down all your wants and needs. No one else has to see your list. If some things are very private, put them down in code. And make sure you dream big – at least one size bigger than you are normally inclined to do. Let your mind run to extremes. Let's face it: Most people dream way too small. When you dream beyond your comfort zone you enlist strategies, plans and tactics that are normally outside your sphere of consideration. More success will result. Typically people list things like a big house in the country, a Bentley, sufficient wealth to be secure for a lifetime, health, a new love interest, extensive travel, loyal friends, an interesting career, etc. You want to own a Bugatti? Write it down. Own your own castle? Write it down. Marry an incredibly beautiful woman? Write it down.

Do not feel guilty for wanting a life of abundance. This world is full of honest, hardworking people who are not financially well off. My parents were happy and content, but even so they couldn't do everything they wanted. They never got to see Africa, Egypt, Australia, East Asia, India or the South Pacific, much as they would have liked. An abundance of wealth enables more adventure, success and

> # DO NOT FEEL GUILTY FOR WANTING A LIFE OF ABUNDANCE.

the freedom to enjoy life to the fullest. Health comes first, of course, but wealth is a close second. The fact is, making more money means you can buy the things you want, assist friends and relations, travel, invest in the stock market, get quality healthcare, good food and accommodation, indulge in any hobby that takes your fancy and support favorite charities.

I am most definitely in favor of abundance, especially if the possession of such enables me to be generous. For me, it is crucial that the path to abundance is free and clear of any untoward behavior to others. I want to be liked. I do not want to be involved in anything illegal or hurtful. I want to be thought of as a reasonable person in possession of above-average integrity.

Few people consider that they are making a choice to be lazy or to procrastinate. They have snuggled into that couch of comfort, and nothing will motivate them to wake up, smell the coffee and get to work on a new path to success. Larry Winget, in his very direct and straightforward book, *You're Broke Because You Want to Be* (Gotham Books), says people do what they do because they want to. "Do this little exercise," he says. "Quickly turn your head from side to side. Did you see anyone on either side of you

> ## NEVER SET A GOAL WITHOUT ATTACHING A TIMELINE TO IT.

holding a gun to your head forcing you to do the stuff you are doing?" Larry goes on to state that if no one is forcing you to do it, then you must be doing it because you choose to. Simple stuff, right?

If right now you are happy and 100 percent satisfied with your life, there is no need to read more of this book. If you can honestly say you are already making the money you

TARGET 1

want and living the life of your dreams, have soaring self-confidence and know how to set goals and stay focused, then close it up now and give it to a friend who is climbing the walls in frustration actively searching for a better and richer life. Isn't that why we are here? If you have a passion for life and all it offers, does the quest for self-improvement ever stop? As William F. Buckley said, "I get satisfaction of three kinds. One is creating something, one is being paid for it and one is feeling that I haven't just been sitting on my ass all afternoon."

Once you have established your dream, make sure it is both workable and something you will enjoy partnering with for a considerable length of time. Never set a goal without attaching a timeline to it. (Stay tuned, we will explore this further in Chapter 6.) You must have a genuine interest in your selected project in order for the results to be successful. Making money for the sake of getting financially rich is not enough. Your interest must be above and beyond the dollar return, otherwise your deeper interest will wane and your business will fall into disarray. Your predominant thoughts must always be on your goal, but you do need to have a money consciousness and a strong, if not burning, desire for wealth. After all, if you don't look for it, it won't find you.

With that being said, though, for all the things money can buy you, there are several things it cannot supply. Money cannot buy you health; it can't buy you happiness; it can't buy you true friends and it can't buy you love. Of course everyone knows this, but do they *really* believe the words? The point was brought home for me a few years ago when I was looking for my ideal home. It had to have an indoor and outdoor pool, plenty of acreage for privacy, a pond, stables, an additional guesthouse and a few other "essentials." All dreamy plans, especially for someone who had started his career living in a one-room apartment that could barely hold a single bed and side table, but by this time in my life I had accomplished what could be termed considerable financial success.

After a bit of a search, I finally found my home. It was owned by one of the creators of Trivial Pursuit, an enormously successful trivia game that had become a huge hit all over the world. I had greatly admired the inventor, Chris Haney, who had been a photographer for a Montreal newspaper. He was extremely intelligent, a trivia buff himself, but in spite of the hundreds of millions the game generated he was caught up with alcohol, tobacco and subsequent unhappiness and depression. I realized incredible financial success didn't automatically translate to happiness. Some rich people are happy, some are not happy. That's the reality.

There is one negative to being rich. It is human nature for others to want some of your wealth. When business people suspect your situation, they have a tendency to charge you more for service. Relations and friends may (and I emphasize the word *may*) start to think of you in terms of your financial status rather than your individuality, disposition and character. Personally I have always tried to be kind and generous to people but sometimes friends, relations,

> ## NEITHER A BORROWER
> ## NOR A LENDER BE.
> *- Shakespeare*

acquaintances or people servicing one's property see only dollar bills and their greed gets the better of them. They can't see beyond your wealth.

Over the years I have had people tell me how lucky I am to have a thriving business. They feel that some quirk of fate meant that I had "made it" while they have only met with failure. Then comes the request for money. "Just a loan of course. I will pay you back." Truth is I have made mistakes and loaned people money. Not only did I not get it back, I made an enemy in the bargain. Shakespeare got it right, "Neither a borrower nor a lender be." Today when people outside my sphere of total trust ask to borrow money, I tell them I keep $3,000 aside to lend to people, but unfortunately it's out at the moment!

But I guess I'm jumping ahead of myself here. First you have to make some money before we start worrying about lending it out. Your job right now is to decide what you want. Once you've done that, I'll tell you how to go about obtaining your wish. Come on, it's time to take the reins of your own life and be the best you can be. The rest of your life is going to be an exciting adventure. This is my promise to you.

AIM FOR THE BULL

- Write down all your wants and needs.

- Make sure you dream big!

- Keep your eyes on the prize.

TARGET 2

Make Sure You've Got a Good Shot at Success

Have you and your friends ever decided to do something that turned out to be a miserable experience? And then at the peak of the misery one friend says, "Why did we choose to do this anyway?" Another adds, "I thought you wanted to do it." "No, I thought you did!" Pretty soon it is agreed that no one had really wanted to do what everyone had ended up doing. Sound familiar?

As Henry Ford said, "Thinking is the hardest activity there is to do; that's why so few people engage in it." Most people would rather act than think. After I saw my teaching colleague's rusted-out "new" Ford, I envisioned a similar depressing future for myself. I knew right then that I needed to go home and think of a plan that would help me escape a similar fate. I didn't want to be waking up one day at the age of 65, suddenly asking myself, "Why did I choose to do this, anyway?"

By now I hope you've decided on what you want. The next step, before we go into full-blown action, is to consider a few things to make sure you have a good shot at success.

TARGET 2

Get real. Sit down and take a good, hard look at your goal. Is it attainable? Realistic? What circumstances would have to exist for you to accomplish it? I don't want to put a damper on your aspirations, but there has to be a chance of achieving your goal if you do all the right things. You can't become a boxing champion at 40 if you've never boxed before. You won't be an Olympic gymnast if you are six-foot-five. You won't be a pro basketball player if you are five feet tall. And you won't become a multimillionaire overnight. Be tough with yourself, but try to hold on to a little naiveté. After all, as columnist Doug Larson stated, "Some of the world's greatest feats were accomplished by people not smart enough to know they were impossible."

> ## IF YOU FEEL QUALIFIED TO GO INTO BUSINESS FOR YOURSELF, I SAY, "START NOW!"

Open your mind. George Bernard Shaw is quoted as saying: "The moment we want to believe something, we suddenly see all the arguments for it and become blind to the arguments against it." Before you begin any venture you have to critically appraise your idea and yourself. You must weigh the strong points and weak points of both. If your goal seems too daunting, you had better talk to people who have already done what you want to do. You may discover that some costs are more than you want to pay, or that the venture could disrupt your personal relationships. You have to weigh all the factors. Achieving your dream may not be worth your marriage, your kids or your health.

Build solid ideas and proceed slowly. Once you have decided to follow a certain path to success don't make a blind rush to the finish line. A starting entrepreneur should know or at least have a very good idea of what he or she is doing. One way of building a good base is to look around you at situations that are similar to what you are considering. Weigh the odds, seek advice and consider the pros and cons of your plan.

You have to learn as much as humanly possible about any activity of investment or entrepreneurship before diving in. Too many people go charging into business ventures on a whim, or in a burst of enthusiasm, or on the advice of some fast-talking salesman. Those who follow a get-rich-quick moneymaking scheme often burn out and fail in double-quick time. Over the years I have known several individuals who have been left money from their parents (or in one case, a friend who won $1.6 million), taken that money and started a business without having more than a slight idea of what that particular business was about. In every case they lost their seed money.

TARGET 2

Be curious. Ask questions before going into action wearing a blindfold. Don't be afraid of seeming too ignorant or needy. Most people will be delighted to give you advice. As Donald Trump wrote in *Think Like a Champion,* "If I'd started in business thinking I knew everything, I'd have been sunk before I started … Never think of learning as being a burden or studying as being boring. It may require some discipline, but it can be an adventure. It can also prepare you for a new beginning." Study and learn from achievers of great magnitude – people like Robert F. Kennedy, who restated George Bernard Shaw's eloquent statement, "Some men see things as they are and say, 'Why?' I dream of things that never were and say, 'Why not?'"

Roll up your sleeves. Thomas Edison said, "Opportunity is missed by most people because it is dressed in overalls and looks like work." If you have an idea for your own business, it's a good idea to gain experience by getting a job with a company in the field of your considered choice. Note that in a large company you may, as an executive, learn and experience only one phase (or maybe two) of the business operations. However, in a small company you are more likely to learn about the overall operation and develop into a seasoned all-rounder, something that will give you a great advantage when you head out on your own.

Stick with it. Jack Canfield, co-creator of *Chicken Soup For The Soul,* reminds us in *The Success Principles* (Harp-

TARGET 2

er Collins) that when a NASA rocket takes off from Cape Canaveral it has to use a huge amount of fuel to break away from the Earth's gravity, but once in space hardly any effort is needed to get to its target destination. The same can be true for the athlete who, after many lonely, penniless years, finally wins a gold medal and gets to see all the endorsement contracts come rolling in.

> # OPPORTUNITY IS MISSED BY MOST PEOPLE BECAUSE IT IS DRESSED IN OVERALLS AND LOOKS LIKE WORK.
> *– Thomas Edison*

My wife, Tosca Reno, is also like that NASA rocket. When she started writing about the importance of "eating clean," no one knew who she was. She spent many lonesome days and nights at the kitchen table planning and testing recipes, pounding the keyboard, coordinating food photographers and stylists … you name it. At times I knew it was difficult for her, but she never complained, never doubted her future success and, most importantly, she never gave up. When you feel so passionately about something, it can be discouraging to keep encountering obstacles in your quest to share it with the world, but here's a testament to the power of hard work and perseverance: Today Tosca has sold over two million copies of books from her *Eat-Clean Diet*® series and they continue to sell at a rate of anywhere from 3,000 to 8,000 per week.

So, if, after taking all of this advice into careful consideration, you feel qualified to go into business for yourself, I say, "Start now!" There are more opportunities than ever before in the history of the world, in hundreds of fields. Check every aspect and then when all is done, go for it. You have made a considered assessment so there's no turning back. Men and women who are beginners today will make large fortunes in the coming years. Let no one dissuade you. Boundless opportunities await. Gentle persistence will pay off.

AIM FOR THE BULL

- Ask yourself if your goals are realistic and achievable. Answer honestly.

- Don't rush. Learn as much as you can about the area of business you intend to enter – and enjoy the learning process!

TARGET 3

Get Off the Darned Couch!

My Austrian father, a ski instructor in Kitzbuhel, Tyrol, for 10 years and then a schoolteacher until he was 80, didn't make a habit of delivering advice on a daily basis, but I do recall he was emphatic that I never, ever break a promise. "Your word is your bond," he would say. "Never be a letdown."

His advice must have stuck because I have always lived by this rule when dealing with others, but also when dealing with myself – especially in regard to my efforts to succeed. Whether I've promised myself I'll start that new magazine I've been mulling over or I've promised my wife I'll pick up the dry cleaning, I always follow through and finish the job when I said I would finish it – or earlier. I don't procrastinate and therefore I'm never a letdown.

Procrastination is one of the most common causes of failure. Many people just cannot get going with their dreams. They are unable to tear themselves away from the TV, the Internet or the daily demands of life. They can't get off the darned couch! The truth is, procrastination is idleness and to me there are few greater sins. What about the idle rich, you say? I don't think so! To quote Richard Templar,

TARGET 3

insightful author of *The Rules of Wealth* (Prentice Hall), "The rich have one thing in common ... they work their socks off. The one thing they all share is the ability to do more in a day than most of us do in a month." Unlike procrastinators, the rich *have* found the time to clean off the kitchen table and get down to planning their future.

I know it sounds harsh, but most people are too lazy to be successful. Have you ever compared the condition of a house that's lived in by a family of individuals who choose not to work for a living with a home that is lived in by a family who choose to be actively engaged in working? There are some interesting contrasts and, yes, some of them are money related (for example, perhaps the unemployed family can't afford a new coat of paint), but several of them aren't. The working family, even though their 9-to-5 jobs take up the bulk of their day, somehow finds time to pull out the weeds, pick up the trash, wash the windows and mow the lawn. It's all a matter of pride. Naturally, not all unemployed people are lazy, but more often than not people with time on their hands become slothful and indolent, whereas busy people find time to be even more industrious.

Barring freak accident or uninvited illness, our destiny is not by chance. It is by choice. You either control your mind or it controls you. The quality of your thinking determines the quality of each day. There is no greater influence on your life's success. Your achievements depend on it. Reportedly one of the definitions of madness is the person who repeatedly does the same thing over and over again, expecting a different result. If you keep parroting past behaviors then you can expect to achieve only what you achieved previously. You can be what you want if you take charge and will it to be.

> IF YOU KEEP PARROTING
> PAST BEHAVIORS
> THEN YOU CAN EXPECT
> TO ACHIEVE ONLY
> WHAT YOU ACHIEVED
> PREVIOUSLY.

An abundance of willpower and discipline is your key to getting started and keeping on track until success is in the bag. Willpower permits you to do what you decided to do, when you said you would do it. I love the line attributed to Napoleon Hill, "Tell me how you spend your spare time and I will tell you where and what you will be 10 years from now." Does this scenario sound familiar? You may think you're just popping onto the Internet to do your banking, but two hours later you've posted several messages on Facebook, read an interesting but random news story and then somehow found yourself browsing through toys from your childhood on eBay. We are all guilty of wasting time. Part of the problem is that time can be so easily wasted. We blink a couple of times and we're into our teens, two more eye blinks and we're looking 30 squarely in the face. One more and we're middle-aged and before we know it we're waking up in an old-age home, awash in a sea of regret. Don't put a hold on your decision to act. Don't postpone joy. See yourself as you want to be and then without hesitation get to work and run your own race.

You've heard the phrase, "use it or lose it." It applies to just about everything involving us humans. If you were bedridden for an extended period of time, your supporting musculature would atrophy and wither away. Non-use always means decay. Use means growth and achievement. Use your brain: read, think, plan and act. Work those brain cells. They long to be activated. As Charles Schulz said, "Life is like a ten-speed bicycle. Most of us have gears we never use." I say, once you get those gears jumping into action, the benefits to your future successful life will snowball like crazy.

I know it's easy for me to sit here and say, "Just do it," but if you are a procrastinator, it is a good idea to think about and address the root causes of your procrastination. Are you afraid of failure? Daunted by an overwhelming task? Disorganized? Easily bored? Confused about your priorities? Most procrastination is related to irrational beliefs.

TARGET 3

What you need to do is confront and challenge these beliefs. The enemy of procrastination is self-discipline. Don't wait for the "right time" to start (because it will never arrive) – just dive in. Often once you do get started, you'll realize the task at hand is not as difficult or scary as you thought – in fact, I'm positive you'll end up enjoying it! Adopt an adventurous attitude.

Think about it. Which of the following tasks is going to get you closer to your dream of living an abundant life: sitting there jotting down the next steps in your action plan or lounging on the couch watching *Two and a Half Men* reruns? The choice is yours!

AIM FOR THE BULL

- Think about why you have not achieved the abundant life you dream of. Confront these irrational beliefs and conquer them.

- There won't always be a tomorrow, so get started on improving your life NOW!

TARGET 4

Don't Wait for Inspiration

A friend of mine used to work for Tony Robbins, and she confirmed my own observations: He is an amazing speaker. If you've ever been to one of his seminars, or one by Zig Ziglar, Stephen Covey or others, you have probably noticed that when the talk is over, a large portion of the audience will be so motivated that they'll be punching the air and whooping with joy, saying things like, "Yeah! I'm gonna do it! I'll change my life, become a huge success and make millions of dollars." Yet if you were to check in with them after a few days or weeks, I'm willing to bet their excitement would have somehow dissolved into thin air and they would most likely be settled back into their old, not-so-successful lives. Don't let this happen to you!

Now, I don't know if you're quite at the fist-pumping stage yet, but at this point in the book, I'm hoping you've written down your major goal, conquered your procrastination issues and that you're excited at the idea of investing your time and efforts into your plan. If in the past you have failed to act on your dreams, now is the time to affirm in your mind that this is it. Repeat the following to yourself: *"Now I will take positive steps to achieve my desire. I will not let myself down. My success is assured."*

TARGET 4

The best strategy, once you've decided on your goal, done your research and looked at your strengths and weaknesses, is to dive in. No excuses. Everyone has a busy life taking kids to school or soccer practice, doing housework, mowing the lawn, taking care of work responsibilities, going to school plays, visiting relatives, paying bills and so on. Don't live under the delusion that successful people were able to achieve their dreams because they didn't have these obligations – in many cases they faced more obstacles than the average person!

> ## THE SECRET OF GETTING AHEAD IS GETTING STARTED.
> *– Mark Twain*

Think of all the excuses Harry Potter® author J.K. Rowling could have made – but didn't. She was a newly divorced single mother on welfare who spent her days caring for her baby daughter, looking for work, trying to get her teaching certification and writing her novel. Because Rowling had such a burning desire to get that story out of her, she didn't make excuses; she made the time to write. She'd write early in the morning, late at night and even in cafés with her daughter sleeping by her side in her stroller. Once the manuscript was finished and typed up (on a

TARGET 4

typewriter!), Rowling had to type it a second time because she couldn't afford to get it photocopied.

The secret to achieving your dream is to understand that despite all the chores and responsibilities, the best time to begin is the present. Mark Twain put it in eight simple words: "The secret of getting ahead is getting started." You can't cross the ocean by merely staring at the waves. A wish without appropriate action is just that: a wish, a dream, a hope. Nothing comes from simply wishing. Action is needed, but the right type of action. Follow your plan to the letter and never stop driving forward.

Replace your fears with those same guts I talk about in the introduction of this book and just go for it. As Kent Sayre wrote in *Unstoppable Confidence!* (McGraw-Hill), "If you want to do something well, it's worth doing poorly at first." You may feel this sounds a little weird, but when you think about it, it makes sense. When you take action you either succeed or don't succeed at first. However, when you don't succeed you will have learned what not to do next time. If fear and laziness are preventing you from taking action, you will learn nothing. You'll be stuck in the same situation you faced in the first place.

Because of my dual occupations as a publisher and oil painter, which keep me immensely busy throughout the day, I get up at 4 a.m. every morning to squeeze in three

TARGET 4

extra hours of work before breakfast. My wife Tosca Reno has the same schedule when writing her *Eat-Clean Diet*® books. Do we grumble at these seemingly insane hours of work time? No way. We work because we like to. No, that's not true. We work because we totally *love it!* And I know that if you think hard and choose wisely, you will find yourself in a similar situation.

> ## WE WORK BECAUSE WE LIKE TO. NO, THAT'S NOT TRUE. WE WORK BECAUSE WE TOTALLY *LOVE IT!*

Whatever you do, don't wait for the "perfect" time to get started. This is just another excuse, and I can detail quite a long list of acquaintances and friends who have become enthused over scripting a play, inventing a board game, starting a business or writing a book, yet who have not managed to actually get their projects underway. They often delayed their projects only to later learn that another person has come up with a similar idea and has reached the finish line before they did. I have made this mistake myself in the past. Remember, there is no 100 percent perfect time to start something new.

TARGET 4

I like what Jack Canfield wrote in *The Success Principles* (Harper-Collins): "Most people are familiar with the phrase 'Ready, aim, fire!' The problem is that too many people spend their whole life aiming and never firing." You just cannot wait for ideal circumstances. How many times have we heard individuals proclaim, "I am just waiting for inspiration"? They could be waiting for years!

> ## START SMALL, BUT START NOW.
> *- Peter H. Thomas*

Start now, even in the smallest way, and continue each day to do something toward attaining your major objective. In his book, *Be Great* (Wiley), Peter H. Thomas, founder of Century 21 Real Estate Canada and LifePilot, wrote five simple words that can determine your life's accomplishments: "Start small, but start now." In other words, once you have put your plan in place, you must do something positive - some *real* action this very day, however small - toward the achievement of that goal. It may be that you just look up information on your computer, buy a few books on the subject you have selected or seek out experts to interview.

TARGET 4

The most important moment is now. It is time for you to clear off the kitchen table, roll up your sleeves and get to work. This will be the most exciting day of your life. Don't waste it.

AIM FOR THE BULL

- Don't let laziness or fear of failure hold you back.

- Don't wait for the ideal circumstances – the best time to start is now.

- No excuses!

- Complete at least one real action *today* that will take you closer to achieving your goal.

TARGET 5

Standing Still is Not an Option

When I entered my teens, I still enjoyed reading comics. At the back of those comics was usually a Charles Atlas advertisement, something along the lines of: *"Don't be a 97-pound weakling. Let me prove I can build you a body to be proud of in just seven days."* Well, I was a pretty smart kid, so I knew you couldn't build a body like that in seven days, but what I didn't realize is that when you *do* build a body like that it doesn't stay built. You have to train regularly if you want to keep looking jacked. Makes sense, right? If you don't commit to a physique-improvement program, your body will lose its strength, contour and fitness level.

The same goes for your self-improvement program. If you don't work at it regularly, you'll end up like those Tony Robbins fans I mentioned in the previous chapter: excited at first, but back to their old habits after a few days. If you want to fulfill your dreams and create more abundance and fun in your life, you have to stick with the program (and yes, it will take longer than seven days). To achieve and be happy you have to keep growing by continuing to accomplish increasingly challenging and rewarding tasks. Standing still is not an option.

TARGET 5

Whether you're building a new body or a new life, hard work and perseverance win through. You may not reach your goals on the first try, but you will succeed if you keep on keeping on. No surrender. That's the secret. I usually get to my office around 10 in the morning and leave at 4 p.m. I'm sure some of my employees think I'm a rich, lazy son of a bitch, but what they don't see is that when I get home I start my *real* workday, often laboring until midnight or beyond and then waking up at 4 a.m. to start all over again. I never want to stand still. I just have no interest in lethargy. I am financially solid, and even though I don't have to work any more, I still choose to. If you are fantasizing about the day you can finally throw in the towel and give up on the working world, be my guest. Retirement is a great joy to many people. It's just not for me. I cannot squander time. I need daily challenge and I'm happy to have that as part of my physical and mental makeup.

> ## NO SURRENDER.
> ## THAT'S THE SECRET.

Most people who make something of their lives, whether through sports, helping others, achieving relationship goals or obtaining financial abundance, do so with lots of hard work. As Richard Templar suggests in *The Rules of Wealth* (Prentice Hall): "You have to work hard, slog your

TARGET 5

guts out, start early, work late. Don't watch TV, waste time [or] take long lunch breaks. Work your socks off."

So, I think by now we've established that hard work is essential to your success. This doesn't mean that you should work hard at just anything, though. We all know people who put in all kinds of hard work their entire lives, and

> WHATEVER DOOR YOU CHOOSE TO OPEN, WHATEVER YOUR SECRET DREAM OR AMBITION, YOU SHOULD NEVER TOTALLY RELAX. SEIZE THE DAY AND TAKE YOUR EFFORTS TO NEW HEIGHTS.

yet they have failed to achieve happiness, satisfaction or financial security. You have to work hard at the important things. Do not waste time on the odds and ends that are relatively unimportant. W. Clement Stone said, "Keep your mind on your objective, and persist until you succeed. Study, think and plan."

TARGET 5

And while you're planning, keep your eye not just on the present but also on the next rung of the ladder. Get excited about moving up. Never settle for the status quo. Where will you be 10 years from now? Think about and commit to your goals, but also try to remain flexible in the face of adversity. Sometimes when all is going well, circumstances can change. Success can become failure. It happens. The answer, as you may have guessed, is to jump back into the fray. Get busy. Rebuild. You can do it. Failure or defeat is only short term. When you get back to fighting in positive territory, your whole life will change for the better. Realize too that with every negative occurrence and every adversity there comes a seed of equivalent advantage. As Alexander Graham Bell said, "When one door closes, another opens; but we often look so long and so regretfully upon the closed door that we do not see the one which has opened for us."

Whatever door you choose to open, whatever your secret dream or ambition, you should never totally relax. Seize the day and take your efforts to new heights. Keep your brain involved. Learn more each day about your target goals. Be bold and proactive. You cannot wait around for things to happen. Napoleon Hill had it right: "Move with decision and promptness and time will favor you. Hesitate or stand still and time will wipe you off the board."

TARGET 5

Now more than ever, change is becoming the most compelling force in our culture. Embrace it and use it to your advantage. As a photographer, one of my main regrets is that I failed to welcome the digital age with open arms. I resisted digital cameras, steadfastly sticking to film for several years. And I know exactly why. I was fearful of not being able to understand the new technology. I knew how to use film, but I recall thinking, 'This new digital stuff is beyond me.' Well, I finally took the plunge and I'm sorry I didn't do so sooner. Film? What's that?

The rate at which technology is advancing and the powerful ways in which it influences our lives can be pretty intimidating. It's hard to keep up with each new innovation; they seem to appear every time we turn around. As entrepreneur, writer and futurist Ray Kurzweil said, "The progress in the 21st century will be about 1,000 times greater than in the 20th century, which was no slouch in terms of change." Keeping up with and adapting to these advancements can sometimes be a struggle, but we can't turn our backs on progress. It doesn't take a genius to figure out if we keep doing the same things day after day, without welcoming new methods, systems or techniques, then we are likely going to be left in the dust as the rest of the world moves ahead. Welcome sensible change. Step it up and dig deep. Remain on hold and success will surely fall away.

TARGET 5

Need another way to avoid standing still? Try creating new income streams. Most wealthy people make money in a variety of ways. Donald Trump didn't rely on Trump Tower as his only source of income, Oprah branched out from a talk show into a multimedia empire, and Richard Branson certainly would have been in trouble if he had never expanded beyond his initial record store. Making your money work for you is a way of maintaining a high level of productivity while also avoiding the many eggs, one basket situation.

> ## WELCOME SENSIBLE CHANGE.

There's a temptation that occurs when we have a success. We are tempted to rest on our laurels. If an investment works out, we have a social success, reach a longed-for goal or realize a business ambition, then some of us feel we can slow down a bit and take it easy. Unfortunately, nothing causes quicker demise than resting on your laurels. When he was only 14, legendary investor Warren Buffett used the profits from his paper route to buy some farmland, which he leased out to local farmers. Shortly after this he and a friend bought a pinball machine and put it in a barbershop. They then used the money made by that machine to go buy a few cases of beer and a new motorcycle.

TARGET 5

No, no, if they had done that, I'm sure that's where Warren Buffett's story would have ended. Instead, Buffett and his friend used the money to buy more pinball machines. And, of course, in just a short time these machines were pulling in profits from all over town.

Remember that possibilities abound. Success can be achieved with consistent planning and effort. And you can build on current success by becoming a possibility thinker. Don't dismiss anything as impossible until you have thoroughly checked it out. As Napoleon Bonaparte said, "The word 'impossible' is not in my dictionary." Make sure it's not in yours either. Keep moving. Never stand still. Life is only truly satisfying when we are growing, learning and achieving on a daily basis.

AIM FOR THE BULL

- Work your socks off, but make sure you're working on what's important.

- Learn as much as you can each day.

- Persist until you succeed, and then keep going. Never stand still.

TARGET 6

Create a Game Plan for Success

How is that inbox on your desk these days? Are your daily meetings, emails, phone calls and paperwork keeping you so busy that you don't even have a moment to crawl out from under the chaos of your cluttered desk to gasp for air?

Getting through your day-to-day work can be a thankless job that is never completed, leaving you with hardly any time or energy to make a plan for your entrepreneurial dreams. The best way to start is during your spare time. Make your plan at home in the evening, on a weekend, while traveling by plane, on vacation, or even early in the morning before breakfast when all is quiet in the home.

In my early 20s, when I came home each day after teaching art at a technical college, I would undo my tie, throw off my jacket, grab a beer, turn on the TV and flop down on the couch … Okay, I'm kidding! I would undo my tie, throw off my jacket, roll up my sleeves, clear off the kitchen table, and get down to work. But I loved it because I had a vision and I was acting on it. And in no way could I describe this activity as work. It was exciting, challenging and fruitful. Only one small notch below sheer unadulterated joy!

TARGET 6

We all want and wish, but now is the time to act by starting with a game plan. A plan is like a road map. It helps you get from A to B. A plane cannot take to the air without a flight plan. It would just cruise around in the sky, lost.

You have to have a plan. It could be that you save 10 percent of your income for that far-off day when you retire. Or you may want to compete in a triathlon, open a restaurant or take your daughter to Paris. Whatever it is, you have to commit to a plan.

Millions of people go through life in misery and poverty because they failed to take the trouble to make a sound plan. The most intelligent person on Earth cannot succeed in any undertaking through his or her own efforts without first building a plan that is practical and workable. The beauty of total commitment to a game plan is that you no longer have any decisions to make. You have decided on your path. You are 100 percent committed. This is where you score over the rest.

Most people have no game plan for life, work or success. They haven't even thought about it. And that's why they fail. With no roadmap for your future you simply end up where the current takes you. Remember, individuals who enjoy great success are not born with some peculiar quality of genius not possessed by others – they just know how to plan, and they follow through with those plans.

TARGET 6

Follow these guidelines to create a five-year, one-year and short-term plan. Right now is a great time to make a new plan.

Your Five-Year Plan

This might be your ultimate goal. The next two plans will help bring you to this extended plan for ultimate achievement. Most people don't plan to fail; they fail to plan. Don't be one of them.

Your One-Year Plan

Think of what you will need to achieve over the next 12 months to bring you to your five-year plan. Post this plan on a wall in your home.

Your Short-Term Plan

This should be your target for achievement in three to six months to get you on your way to achieving your long-term goal. Because of the short period, your plan has to be especially workable and achievable.

As the old saying goes, "A journey of a thousand miles begins with a single step." When creating your game plan for success, the important thing is that the first step is made with careful consideration and that it is in the right direction. Napoleon Hill told literally tens of thousands who attended his seminars that to be successful in any kind of endeavor, one must have a definite goal toward which to work. You must have a positive plan to achieve your goal.

TARGET 6

He also emphasized that you must work systematically and continuously toward achieving your goal, every day.

Thoughts truly are powerful things. Put them into a written plan and presto! You are on your way. A plan is really no more than putting your hopes and desires into an orderly arrangement. Plan your work, and work your plan. There is little doubt that those who achieve greatness make a habit of obsessing over their major definite purpose. You succeed at what you think about all day.

Richard Templar writes in *The Rules of Work* (Prentice Hall): "Developing a game plan is a bit like an actor choosing a part and learning a script. Your game plan has to be who you are going to be." He adds that not many people actively choose to be a loser, but that's where they end up.

> THOUGHTS TRULY ARE
> POWERFUL THINGS. PUT
> THEM INTO A WRITTEN
> PLAN AND PRESTO! YOU
> ARE ON YOUR WAY.

Be fearless when making your plan. Don't sell yourself short. The more daring your vision, the larger your potential for success. Remember that most serious planners achieve their goals and go on to make even more daring

TARGET 6

game plans as time goes on. Don't be frightened to plan to go all the way. You could be in line for outrageous success, especially if you act as though your plan is already real.

Richard Carlson, Ph.D. says in *Don't Sweat the Small Stuff About Money* (Hyperion), "The implications of thinking big are widespread and impressive." You can think small or you can think big. Give me your answer now. What's it going to be? Thinking big makes your life a lot easier and a lot more fun. Make sure you incorporate some big goals when you make your game plan for your future. After all, it is your life, right?

AIM FOR THE BULL

- Plan your work, and work your plan. Start now by creating five-year, one-year and short-term plans.

- Don't sell yourself short.

- Immerse yourself in the role you've created.

TARGET 7

Fill a Need and You Will Fill Your Bank Account

When Jean Paul Getty spoke of giving people what they want, he probably didn't have the Snuggie in mind. Nevertheless, as I write this I have just learned that sales of this much-ridiculed blanket with sleeves have surpassed the $100 million mark. Now, whether you attribute the Snuggie's success to the fact that its cheesy ads became the butt of several talk-show jokes, which propelled it to the mainstream, or the fact that it was a comforting product that was marketed as a way to help reduce heating bills, there's no disputing that this "Pet Rock of the Depression 2.0 era" (as *The New York Times* called it) offered people something they wanted in difficult times.

Now it's your turn to think about what interests you most in life – and how you can parlay it into something people need. Don't choose something you know little about just because you have heard there's a bunch of money to be made. Choose a product or service that you have an affinity for and are knowledgeable about. What's your hobby? Golf, blogging, bird watching, writing, tarot cards, tattoos, fishing, fashion, running? Now think of a way it can be improved. How can you help people become better anglers, bloggers and so on? Remember my adventures in taxidermy? Think about how your fellow hobbyists could benefit from better skills, clothing, trainers or accessories. Is there a need for instructional manuals, books, CDs or DVDs? Although it is becoming increasingly difficult to stand out in the more than 12 hours of video uploaded to YouTube each minute, perhaps you can reach the world this way. Train your mind to be constantly exploring opportunities.

> ## HELP OTHERS FIND WHAT THEY WANT, AND YOU WILL GET WHAT YOU WANT.

Underlying everything is the enormously powerful yet simple mantra I introduced in the first few pages of this book: Help others find what they want and you will get all that you want. Jack Canfield says in *The Success Principles* (Harper Collins), "Find a way to serve." (And he's not talking about tennis here, although being great at that sport is most definitely one way to enter the millionaire club.) Serving others, whether by helping out charities, working with the underprivileged or finding some small way to improve people's lives, will always come back to you multiplied. It's the way of the universe.

TARGET 7

Which brings us to the second part of the mantra: Give people what they want *and you will get all that you want.* Of course, money should not be your main motive for helping others, but we can't deny it's likely what drove you to pick up this book. Maybe you're too young to remember Bing Crosby, but you no doubt have heard him at some point. Among other tunes, he would croon about swinging on a star and being better off than you are. Who wouldn't want that? It's human nature. Now "better off" can be interpreted in many ways: healthier, happier, free of stresses and worry, fitter, younger looking or – let's be blunt here – in possession of an abundance of cold, hard cash.

> MONEY ISN'T EVERYTHING,
> BUT IT'S RIGHT UP THERE
> WITH OXYGEN.
>
> *- Zig Ziglar*

Money is a wonderful thing. It can't buy you health, love or even happiness, but it is the commodity that can buy you the toys – a house in the country, cars, clothes, planes, boats – you name it. It can also buy you the luxury and joy of travel. And in my frequent travels, I've talked to those who have money, those who don't and those who've had it and lost it. As you can probably guess, the general con-

TARGET 7

sensus is that a life with money is more satisfying than one without it. Inspirational speaker Zig Ziglar puts it another way: "Money isn't everything, but it's right up there with oxygen."

Getting wealthy is the aim of many people. It is competitive. It is also very rewarding and most definitely exciting and attainable if you're willing to follow the rules, work smart and work hard. If you've been paying attention so far, you already know that hard work is essential to becoming super wealthy. But what may seem like hard work to you now as you read this is definitely going to become a daily joy as you accumulate those dollar bills. You will in time develop a complete absence of money worries.

When you have decided how to make your fortune and have set your plan of action, I strongly suggest that you strengthen that plan by adding emotion to the strategy. In other words, if you want to make a certain amount of money during the coming year, attach a reason for wanting that money: a longed-for trip to Tahiti, a European vacation for your parents, a Bentley convertible, anything that's important to you. Women who find it hard to diet usually have an easier time of it if they think of that coming vacation where they will be wearing a bikini on the beach. The same goes for celebrities who want to look good on the red carpet or in their next film. I will go into further detail on the importance of emotionalizing your wishes in Chapter 12.

TARGET 7

In this pursuit of a life of abundance, you need to aim at being the best at what you do. Second best is not an option. Expect success. Give thought to the plan we talked about in the previous chapter. Every day you should do at least three things that contribute to the fulfillment of your plan. If you are currently a wage earner, give more to your efforts. Render more service than you promise. Develop your own moneymaking plan, clean off that kitchen table when you get home and sweat it out. Yes, the main obstacle is getting started – as the philosopher Horace said, "He who has begun is half done" – *but* it is also important to build momentum, and keep it going. Letting go even once can lead to the death of your project. It's like the person who's trying to diet or stop smoking: one puff of a cigarette can lead back to that pack-a-day habit. One chocolate-covered doughnut can be the catalyst that returns you to your habit of daily junk food binges. You always have to be thinking of and preparing for your next moves.

Believe it or not, I learned this the hard way. Quite some time ago, I decided I would invent a board game and make millions of dollars. I cleared the kitchen table and worked away on it for a couple of days. On the third day my wife needed the table so we cleared off everything and tossed it into a cupboard. Out of sight, out of mind. The momentum was lost and I never got back to the board game. Meanwhile, the inventors of Trivial Pursuit kept on keeping on

TARGET 7

and eventually hit the big time with sales of more than 100 million copies in over 25 countries.

With that being said, I'm not going to pretend that running your own business is a shoo-in to millions of dollars. When it comes to failure rates for startup companies, let's just say that if your business hasn't tanked within the first five years you are in a very *low* percentile. Failure is often due to narrow, limited thinking. Was money the sole reason for starting your business? That's not enough. There has to be more to it.

> *YOUR* BUSINESS IS NOT GOING TO FAIL BECAUSE YOU ARE GOING TO GO THE EXTRA MILE.

Laziness and lack of interest in the business itself can also lead to failure. How many times have you waited for a bank teller when there are two or three empty wickets and several people behind the counter doing nothing? How often have you entered a store where everything was a jumble of random items, there was dust everywhere and even the service was dismal? You were not greeted with a smile and a solid "Let me know if I can be of help." No sir, the woman behind the counter was on the phone with her girlfriend yakking about the hot guy she met the night before.

TARGET 7

I know that *your* business is not going to fail because you are going to go the extra mile. You will care passionately about the product (or service) and the customer. You will be continuously planning your next successes and anticipating roadblocks. It's Newton's first law: An object in motion stays in motion. Nothing will stop you, and before you know it the world will be beating a path to your door.

There are millions, yes millions, of ways to make money, but right now your job is to get started on the path to making money – an abundance of money. Remember what America's most successful inventor said. "I never perfected an invention that I did not think about in terms of service it might give to others. I find out what the world needs, then I proceed to invent it." Okay, so Edison tied up the incandescent electric light bulb, but believe me, there are a million more needs created daily that require thoughtful attention. Identify a need that isn't being met, and plan how you will meet it. Your financial abundance is around the corner. Now go and enrich your life.

TARGET 7

AIM FOR THE BULL

- Train your mind to be constantly considering opportunities and possibilities.

- Choose a product or service that you have an affinity for and think of a way it can be improved.

- Do at least three things each day that contribute to the fulfillment of your plan.

TARGET 8

Marketing: It's the Secret for Guaranteed Results

As you might have guessed, I am not just an advocate of business entrepreneurship – I have successfully involved myself in numerous business ventures, which continue to bring in almost one million dollars each week. Despite my continued success, I'm always willing to learn. In fact, I have spent a great deal of time immersing myself in the work of such life success experts as Jim Rohn, Tony Robbins, Zig Ziglar, Bob Proctor, Joe Vitale, Stephen Covey, Wayne Dyer and others. I attend talks and seminars when possible, and my home library contains scores of books that deal with successful living and getting what we want

IF YOU WANT YOUR
PRODUCT OR SERVICE
TO BE A SUCCESS,
PEOPLE HAVE TO KNOW
WHO YOU ARE AND
WHAT YOU ARE DOING.

TARGET 8

out of this short stretch of time we call life. However, many of these otherwise helpful resources fail to talk about the importance of marketing.

One man who does give enormous credence to marketing is Ernie J. Zelinski, author of *Career Success Without a Real Job* (Ten Speed Press). Ernie gets right down to brass tacks. He writes, "The difference between a best-selling product or service and a bomb is marketing strategy. ... I can't give enough ink to the fact that marketing is the mother, father, grandmother, aunt and uncle too, of extraordinary success attained with any product or service." Brilliant!

But what exactly is marketing? It is the projection of your product or service to the marketplace. If you want your product or service to be a success, people have to know who you are and what you are doing. It is not enough to complete your job and hope for the best. Believe me, as you'll learn from the mistakes I describe below, marketing is not about being modest!

Although I now know without a doubt that big promotion pays off big, I wasn't always aware of this basic truth. Back in the '80s, a young wannabe magazine publisher approached me for advice about the magazine business. He wanted to learn whatever he could about magazine production, distribution and sales. I told him everything I knew, and in a short period of time Bill Phillips became successful in the magazine business. We then both went into book publishing.

In order to sell my book *Bodybuilding for Women* (Emerson Books), I mentioned it once in my magazine, *MuscleMag International*. The book went down the drain, selling a mere few thousand copies. Meanwhile, Bill Phillips mentioned his book *Body for Life* on almost every page of his magazine, complete with countless images of the book's cover, before-and-after photographs of men and women who had used the book to lose weight and several pictures of Bill himself.

I can distinctly recall making disdainful remarks to my staff about this outrageous marketing blitz that seemed to me like the epitome of cheap and vulgar over-promotion. I changed my tune, however, when I saw that within the first year of the book's release, Bill's *Body for Life* had sold almost three million copies.

Although the book business has changed dramatically since then, it is still virtually impossible for an unknown author to have a successful book without solid marketing behind it. This goes for every business venture or service you may choose to follow. My wife Tosca Reno is a natural when it comes to marketing. Thanks to her tireless efforts, including countless book signings, personal appearances, Facebook chats, radio and TV interviews and more, her

Eat-Clean Diet® book series has sold in huge numbers, so much so that one big New York publisher offered $500,000 just for the rights to republish her books. When we refused, the offer was doubled the next day. I must admit, the temptation to accept was there but we still said no. The buzz for Tosca's books kept growing, though, and before we knew it eight of the top publishers in the US participated in an auction for her next work. It turned into a bidding war that was eventually won by Harlequin. The resulting book, *Your Best Body Now,* became a *New York Times* bestseller almost the first week it hit the stores.

In my own career I have enjoyed, and continue to enjoy, creative business activity in retail stores, book publishing, mail order, freelance writing, clothing manufacturing, magazine production, property rental and my own personal oil painting and sculpture. The topic of oil painting actually brings to mind a few marketing misadventures I experienced back when I was promoting my book *Hardcore Bodybuilding*.

I was in New York, slated to appear on six shows in two days. At *The Joe Franklin Show,* which was a live morning show, I was given a seat at a small table and a copy of my book was on the empty seat next to me. It was almost time for the show to start and there was no Joe Franklin in sight. It was quite nerve-wracking as I sat there alone with the cameras pointed at me. At the very last minute, the elevator door opened and out walked Joe. He came over to his chair, picked up my book, flicked through the pages and said, "Mr. Kennedy, what makes a guy like you write a book like this?" I didn't miss a beat and gave some standard answers to his questions.

The next guest on the show was an oil painter who demonstrated how to paint an entire canvas in 32 seconds! Boy, did I look dull in comparison! When I talked to my publicity agent afterwards, he said simply, "You came across like a well-spoken Englishman. I seriously doubt if you sold one book!"

Later that afternoon, I was appearing on another show. Health and wellness writer Joyce Vedral was also there to talk about her diet and exercise book. She jumped on the host's coffee table and started yelling and shouting while holding up a poster-sized photo of her obese daughter. She looked straight at the television camera and yelled: "Check this out. This is my youngest daughter before she followed my book!"

And then, surprise, surprise, she pulled her shy daughter out of the front row and over to the coffee table. "Get up

TARGET 8

> YOU NEED TO LET
> PEOPLE KNOW ABOUT
> YOUR BUSINESS VIA
> TV, RADIO, NEWSPRINT,
> MAGAZINES, SOCIAL
> MEDIA, ADVERTISING,
> SEMINARS, THE INTERNET
> AND WORD OF MOUTH.

here, honey. Show everyone that beautiful body. Check her out folks. Give her a hand. She lost over 50 pounds following the advice in my book!"

I looked at my publicity agent and gave a cynical smile, which I quickly regretted. "Don't laugh," said my agent. "She's selling books!" I had learned my lesson about marketing. From then on I not only mentioned my books, but actively boasted about them.

You need to let people know about your business via TV, radio, newsprint, magazines, social media, advertising, seminars, the Internet and word of mouth. Surprisingly, some of the best ways of spreading the word are the least expensive. If you have a huge marketing budget you can hire a publicity agent (which can run up a monthly bill of $5,000 to $7,000) and an advertising agency, but if you don't have money to spare, a bit of creativity and imagination can go a long way.

> ## ONE OF THE BEST AND LEAST EXPENSIVE WAYS TO GET PUBLICITY IS VIA THE TELEPHONE INTERVIEW WITH RADIO STATIONS BECAUSE YOU DO NOT NEED TO TRAVEL.

In the case of the Vancouver-based junk removal company 1-800-Got-Junk, an invaluable marketing idea was virtually free. Company founder Brian Scudamore emailed *The Oprah Winfrey Show* asking to be featured on any of their home renovation-themed shows. When he didn't hear back, he mailed them a letter. Finally, six months later Scudamore received a call from one of Oprah's producers asking if his company would help clear out a woman's house on a show about hoarding. This led to appearances on *The View* and *Dr. Phil* and these days the company has more than 200 franchises in three countries.

One of the best and least expensive ways to get publicity is via the telephone interview with radio stations because

TARGET 8

you do not need to travel. Don't dismiss small radio stations just because they do not reach many listeners. You never know who's listening, and one show can lead to another. Some other low-budget marketing options include sending out press releases about your product or service to magazines, newspapers, TV and radio stations, bloggers, etc. (lists are available via the Internet). If you're willing to put in the work and you have an interesting story, you will get noticed.

Another key to marketing success is to understand right from the outset that the people who work in the media have absolutely zero interest in promoting your product, business or service. Their main concern is providing interesting content for their audiences. Accordingly you had better be riveting, entertaining and even controversial, if you want to make an impact. Always remember there are literally hundreds of thousands of people doing the same thing and they are all fighting to be noticed. You have to be different. And being different these days is even more important than being better.

When Arnold Schwarzenegger first started to get recognition outside the bodybuilding field, his agent got him on *The Tonight Show* starring Johnny Carson (which had a nightly audience of 20 million North Americans at the time). Arnold's agent warned him that if he didn't put on a good show Johnny would never ask him back on again.

TARGET 8

Accordingly, Arnold worked up a few good stories to keep his audience entertained.

"Tell me, Arnold, what's it like when you are training and you get a muscle pump?" asked Carson.

"It's fantastic," replied Arnold with a wry smile. "It's like sex when you are cumming!"

At this point the women in the audience (and at home) put their hands to their open mouths, shocked – did he *really* say that word?

Arnold continued: "Yes, Johnny, when you pump iron it is truly amazing. And you know something? I train twice a day … so it feels like I'm cumming all day long!"

Arnold had a knack of going right up to the edge on late-night talk shows and, truth be told, the combination of his Austrian accent and youthful good looks granted him an unofficial license to be a little more risqué than other guests. Needless to say Arnold Schwarzenegger was asked to return and to date has made in excess of 25 guest appearances on *The Tonight Show.*

Arnold once told me: "I always take a list of questions with me when I go on radio or TV. Usually the host declines, saying that he'd rather conduct his own interview, to which I

TARGET 8

reply, 'Of course, but I have fantastic answers for my questions that will really hold your audience's attention.'" Invariably, he said, after a minute or two of conversation the host would glance down at the list and start asking the questions Arnold had submitted.

> ## GOOD PUBLIC RELATIONS IS REALLY ABOUT HAVING SOMETHING DIFFERENT TO SAY IN THE FIRST PLACE.
>
> *- Richard Branson*

It's always a good idea to make the job of an editor, producer or host easier by providing them with a great story so they don't have to dig. The more outrageous, passionate and controversial the better. And as we all know only too well Arnold has shown a knack for taking his behavior a little too far for the acceptable level dictated by the general public. As creative billionaire Richard Branson reminds us, "Good public relations is really about having something different to say in the first place." In other words, you must first be able to recognize what's unique about your product and then you need to get the word out to the public as passionately and memorably as possible. Former Chrysler CEO Lee Iacocca said, "You can have brilliant ideas, but if you can't get them across, your ideas won't get you anywhere."

AIM FOR THE BULL

- When it comes to marketing your product, don't be afraid to toot your own horn – no one else will.

- No marketing budget? Get creative! A simple email and letter was all it took to launch Brian Scudamore's company, 1-800-Got-Junk, into the stratosphere.

- Make the interviewer's job easier. The more interesting your story is, the more likely it is to be covered, talked about and remembered.

TARGET 9

Scared Money
Never Wins

When it comes to stress and worry, I tend to agree with Hamlet, who said, "There is nothing either good or bad, but thinking makes it so." Stressed-out people see only the negative side of things. They blow problems way out of proportion. I know it's hard not to worry when a problem comes up - or even when there is no problem but your brain has that annoying habit of creating one (this often happens when you're lying in bed unable to sleep), but stress is something we must strive to conquer. Not only will it interfere with the quality of your business, it can cause problems in your relationships with friends and family.

When you panic, you fail to see things clearly and end up causing bigger problems than you began with. I'm sure at one time or another we've all lost our keys or mislaid the ticket that gets us out of the parking lot. We feel the panic accelerate as we dig through our pockets or bags until we become frantic, searching like a caged animal seeking freedom. Our minds go blank. We lose all logic until we finally collect ourselves, calm down and search with deliberation. It is only when we proceed slowly and methodically that we will ultimately achieve success and find our mislaid items.

TARGET 9

When I was starting to get serious about business, I ended up doing too much by trying to juggle a full-time teaching job with working for myself at night, often into the wee hours. I was experiencing a building anxiety and, as a result, started to get frequent stomachaches. I went to see my doctor. He introduced me to Rolaids and cautioned me that too much stress caused excess acid to seep into my stomach. He said that if I didn't watch out I would develop an ulcer.

My eyes grew wide with the realization that I was in the process of destroying my health. This was enough to make me slow down and take things in stride. I realized that the sources of my anxiety were never going to disappear, so instead I had to change the way I handled them. Now, 40 years later, I deal with problems calmly and rationally. I do not often panic and anxiety is a thing of the past. Best of all, I haven't had a stress-related stomachache since.

Instead of allowing worry to mess up your health, it's far better to face any potential problem head on. When you're feeling anxious, take a few deep breaths and try to tune in to the reality of the situation. As you breathe, ask yourself, Will this really matter a year from now (or next week, five years from now and so on)? Instead of allowing the emotion of outright panic to take hold, endeavor to channel your concern into being cool, calm and collected. This will enable you to apply reasonable and balanced thought to solving your problems.

TARGET 9

> ## WHEN PREPAREDNESS MEETS OPPORTUNITY, SUCCESS IS ASSURED.

Another common cause of anxiety is argument. This can be between colleagues, family members, friends or spouses. Learn to edit your conversation before trouble-instigating words leave your mouth. All too often an argument starts from a careless choice of words. You may not have meant any harm but someone takes your comment the wrong way and trouble ensues. Few things can cause stress more quickly than an accelerating exchange of hostile words. If someone says or does something that pushes your buttons, try to pause for a minute and examine the situation before reacting. Some arguments can be over in minutes, but some can last a lifetime.

If you are the type to worry about being late for work or for an appointment, then rather than advancing the likelihood of a meltdown, try leaving the house 10 minutes earlier than normal. Plan ahead and do whatever you can to avoid creating situations that encourage worry. In fact, anything becomes easier when you have a plan. And when preparedness meets opportunity, success is assured.

A couple of years ago, I gave a lecture on health and fitness to a rather large group of men and women. I wrote out my speech and practiced it on a daily basis for a full week before going onstage. The lecture went well.

The following year I was asked to give a seminar to an audience of personal fitness trainers. I didn't write it out. I didn't plan it. I didn't practice. I thought I knew it all. The audience was somewhat sparse and there was a noisy child right in the front row. I was distracted and a chain reaction took place.

I panicked. My face became flushed and my mind totally blanked! Because I couldn't think of anything to say, I ended up asking the audience for questions, but my situation was compounded because no one in the audience wanted to ask questions. Quite frankly, with all my experience, I was surprised and angry that I could have let this happen. Fortunately, I got through my talk without a real catastrophe. Although my audience may not have noticed much, for me personally it was excruciatingly painful.

> ## THE MAN WHO IS PREPARED HAS HALF HIS BATTLE FOUGHT.
> *- Miguel de Cervantes*

TARGET 9

This year I was again contacted to give a lecture – and I took no chances. I wrote out my speech, placed key headings on small index cards and rehearsed for an hour a day during the week before. As you might guess, all went well.

Let me tell you, there is no substitute for being prepared. My talk couldn't have gone better because the confidence I had from being prepared paid off. I had no worry or anxiety. Spanish novelist Miguel de Cervantes said, "The man who is prepared has half his battle fought." I will never again get up onstage without knowing my subject intimately and in great detail.

Another way to alleviate anxiety is to have some sort of outlet for your frustrations. In his book *Why Zebras Don't Get Ulcers*, biologist and neuroscientist Robert M. Sapolsky describes an experiment with rats and stress, the results of which I found quite intriguing.

In the experiment, the first rat would receive mild electrical shocks over time, causing it to develop a prolonged stress response, which dramatically increased the probability of the rat getting an ulcer. In a separate area, a second rat would get the same series of shocks, but whenever it was shocked, it was allowed to run over to a bar of wood and chew on it. Because the second rat had an outlet for its frustration, it was far less likely to get an ulcer. Interestingly, the same went for the third rat who, after receiving the

TARGET 9

same series of shocks, was less stressed because it was allowed to go across the cage and bite another rat (although I definitely don't recommend this type of displacement of aggression when dealing with your own stress!).

As Sapolsky writes, "We humans also deal better with stressors when we have outlets for frustration – punch a wall, take a run, find solace in a hobby. We are even cerebral enough to *imagine* those outlets and derive some relief: consider the prisoner of war who spends hours imagining a golf game in tremendous detail."

Speaking as a health and fitness publisher, I can't stress enough how effective physical activity is at helping you cope with stress and anxiety. Once you get moving, you are not only making your body stronger and healthier, you are also releasing your frustrations and getting those mood-boosting endorphins pumping. A "runner's high" isn't only for runners! You can achieve the same effects by engaging in any form of strenuous exercise.

Sharing your concerns with a trusted colleague, friend or spouse is also a great way to relieve stress. Don't hold things inside where they can infiltrate your mind and appear more important than they really are. Aim to be tranquil. Use the experience of others to allay your fears. Pay attention to how they handle pressure. Sir Isaac Newton said, "If I have seen far, it is by standing on the shoulders of giants."

TARGET 9

Solicit feedback if you can't handle a problem on your own. You will be surprised at how those who are distanced from your problem can provide sensible solutions that may have eluded you because of your closeness to the situation.

> WE HAVE SO MANY
> THINGS TO FILL OUR
> MINDS, WHY ADD
> THE JUNK THAT
> CAUSES ANXIETY?

Let's learn to relax and kick anxiety to the curb. We need to be realistic in our lives. We have to understand what's important and what's not so important. Doesn't it make sense to avoid stress? We have so many things to fill our minds, why add the junk that causes anxiety?

AIM FOR THE BULL

- Stay cool. Instead of letting stress mess with your health and judgment, take responsibility for your life and face your problems head on.

- Remember the rat experiment! Having an outlet for your frustrations will help you deal with the stressors in your life.

- Talk it out. Sometimes sharing your problems with a friend can help take a load off. Others can often provide new perspectives, making your troubles seem less daunting.

TARGET 10

Apply Faith

When I was learning to be a painter and sculptor at the Norwich School of Art in the UK, I started off as a rather listless worker. A burning desire hadn't yet visited my psyche, and it didn't look as though it was going to visit anytime soon. One day, as I sat there during one of my breaks from hacking away at a block of limestone, my sculpture teacher, Mr. Rowbottom, normally an extremely mild-mannered man, came over to talk to me.

"Having trouble concentrating, Kennedy? Not making great progress with our stone carving, are we?"

"No, Sir," I replied with unacceptable nonchalance.

"Well, for God's sake, Kennedy, you're squandering your time here. Get enthusiastic about your work. You're acting like a damn zombie. Get passionate about your art. Believe in yourself. Otherwise you are wasting your time, my time and your parents' money."

That did it for me. I had never had a teacher talk to me so bluntly. My enthusiasm for any project and for life itself shot up by 1,000 percent! And I've never looked back.

TARGET 10

It's an unmistakable truth that those who win in the game of life are the ones who think they can win. Most people fail not because they lack the skills or aptitude to reach their target, but simply because they don't believe they can do it.

We all suffer from self-doubt at times, but self-doubt is tantamount to self-sabotage. We need to make self-belief a conscious and consistent choice. When we truly believe in ourselves and combine that belief with knowledge of our chosen field along with enthusiasm to act positively, we develop a profound focus that virtually guarantees our success.

It's nice, certainly comforting, to have others believe in you. If parents, friends, coworkers and especially your spouse believe in you and show it, then some of the battle is won. In fact, a few days after Mr. Rowbottom chastised me for not believing in myself, I overheard him telling another teacher that he wished I would apply myself more, because in his opinion I was an extremely gifted artist. This gave me a great boost. I hope that you, too, will get to hear and digest true praise about your amazing abilities. However, with that being said, the most important believer in you is *you*. Belief in yourself is absolutely essential.

It's hard to get people to believe in themselves. Okay, maybe people have faith in themselves on occasion, but that

TARGET 10

belief is not sustainable. We need to turn things around and start believing we can succeed in any venture we put our minds to. How do we do this? We need to examine ourselves and assess who we really are. It's easy to conclude that we know nothing, that there is nothing of value in our heads. It is at such times that we should dig back into our minds and remind ourselves of our past achievements, victories and successes.

> THERE IS OBVIOUSLY
> A HIGHER PLAN FOR YOU.
> AS YOU NOW TAKE
> CHARGE OF YOUR LIFE,
> THAT PLAN WILL, WITH
> YOUR COMMITMENT,
> BE FULFILLED.

Don't allow any meaningful approbation of praise to escape your memory. Hold it intact to keep your self-belief strong and healthy. All things are possible to a person who believes they are possible.

Keep in mind that you have already won the biggest lottery there is. Out of billions of wasted sperm lost to the ages, the one that helped create you made it to fruition, bringing you with deliberation to your current position on

TARGET 10

Earth. There is obviously a higher plan for you. As you now take charge of your life, that plan will, with your commitment, be fulfilled.

We all have the power to believe in ourselves and in our ability to do well in life. To have doubts will minimize our chances. To be truly successful, we need the courage that self-belief brings to both our situations and ambitions. Successful people are driven by their unshakable belief in what they are aiming to accomplish. Their drive forward never lessens until their worthy goal is achieved.

> ## DON'T BE HANDICAPPED BY THINKING OF THINGS YOU CAN'T DO.
> *- Mark Twain*

You've also got to, as Mr. Rowbottom said, "Get passionate about your art." Recultivate that burning desire. A burning desire is a dream that you take to bed with you at night. You eat with it, sleep with it and keep it foremost in your mind. Truth is, you first get it and then it gets you. The passion you have created makes it impossible for you to stop the forward momentum. Your success is assured because the mind attracts that which it feeds upon. Jack Canfield, the amazing creator of *Chicken Soup for the Soul* and *The Success Principles* (Harper Collins), says: "There is growing research that the vibrations of positive expectation that successful people give off actually attract to them the very experiences they believe they are going to get."

"Enthusiasm," said Ralph Waldo Emerson, "is one of the most powerful engines of success." Accordingly, when you undertake a task, do it with every ounce of your being. Put your own signature on it. Stamp it with your very soul and listen to no one who isn't a 100-percent believer in what you are trying to achieve. Trust your original thought.

Einstein said imagination is more important than knowledge. You should spend time daily, even if only for a minute or two, in the practice of creative envisioning. See yourself as a confident, able individual, a person full to the brim with self-belief. Don't allow negative remarks to hurt you, and certainly do not allow them to affect your self-confidence. Many remarks are made out of spite or jealousy and have no substance.

Alter your life by altering your attitude. Out of this will come incredible confidence and self-belief. Your quality of life depends upon the quality of your beliefs. The more empowering your self-belief, the more success you will attract.

TARGET 10

No less an author than Mark Twain said, "Don't be handicapped by thinking of things you can't do." I urge you to do a deep self-search for anything about your belief system that is negative. Ask yourself whether a particular belief serves you. If so, welcome it to the heart of your soul. Other stuff that isn't part of the successful you? Get rid of it with all the skill you can muster.

AIM FOR THE BULL

- Do a deep self-search and assess who you really are.

- Make self-belief a conscious and consistent choice.

- Remind yourself of past achievements, victories and successes.

- Spend time daily, even if only for a minute or two, envisioning yourself as a confident, able individual.

TARGET 11

Don't Let Anyone Talk You Out of Your Vision (or Your Money)

You are reading this book because you want to be somebody. You want to be wealthy, famous, triumphant in love, or all three. You want to learn. Perhaps you want a palatial country home or a 155-foot yacht. Or maybe you want to master a musical instrument, travel the world or climb Mount Everest.

Whatever the case, it can happen only with planning, followed by concrete action fueled by a burning desire and relentless drive to go the extra mile. Then, even if you've checked all those boxes, you still have to watch out for scams and sabotage. They happen more often than you might imagine. What's even worse is that these destructive acts aren't just perpetrated by random con artists and your enemies, but also by friends, relations and even yourself.

I'm sure you've experienced some version of the sabotage I'm talking about. Remember when you wanted to lose a few pounds? Your pants started getting a little tight, so you decided to avoid those sugar-loaded goodies that seem to make their way to most coffee tables. When your friend held the plate up to you, you put up your hand and said, "No thanks, I'm watching my weight." And what was the return communiqué? Did your friend offer words of understanding, admiration and approval? No way. What you got was probably something like "Oh, come on! Just one piece of cake won't hurt you. You can't starve yourself. Go on, take a slice." And what if you gave in and took a slice of that creamy chocolate cake? Chances are, you witnessed a complacent, evil smile.

> **IF YOU FEEL YOU HAVE LIMITING BELIEFS ABOUT ACHIEVING SUCCESS OR WEALTH, THEN THINK BACK TO YOUR EARLY CHILDHOOD.**

Why do those who are supposed to care about us sabotage our higher efforts? In some cases, it is because our success – whether in losing weight, building a business or succeeding in any other chosen endeavor – reminds them that they haven't fulfilled their dreams. In other words, your industry and passion to succeed rubs them the wrong way, forcing them to confront their own laziness. There's an old saying so true you will recognize the accuracy of it immediately: "We want our friends to succeed – but not more than we do." Right on!

Unfortunately, most people never even get to the first stages of achieving their dreams because they sabotage themselves with limiting beliefs that have followed them since childhood. Some people believe that success and affluence are bad for our spiritual growth. My own parents were very much against me endeavoring to make more money than I was earning as a teacher. My father actually believed the opulent among us made their fortunes on the backs of the working class. He had no interest in abundance. He worked hard and got total satisfaction from his hobbies, lawn bowling and chess.

If you feel you have limiting beliefs about achieving success or wealth, then think back to your early childhood and consider what you recall hearing from your parents, grandparents, siblings, aunts and uncles, teachers, religious figures, coworkers and friends. Write down any of the beliefs that you feel may affect your passion to do well.

Let's assume, for example, that you want to be a famous actor, but your parents have repeatedly scorned the acting profession with statements like "Those people are all philandering, narcissistic nut jobs high on alcohol and drugs." Your assignment now is to analyze the veracity of their beliefs. Yes, there are some weirdos in the entertainment industry, but there are also a great many respected actors who have given a lot to society with their magical performances and generosity to various charities.

Combat your limiting beliefs by constantly reminding yourself that they aren't true. Make a promise to yourself and write it down. For the abovementioned example, it could be something like "I will do my utmost to become an extremely accomplished actor and I will avoid the pitfalls of excess such as alcohol, drugs, narcissism and extramarital affairs." Place this promise on your bathroom mirror or someplace else where you will see it frequently.

Here's another form of sabotage you may not have thought of. You can hinder your own efforts by the way you stand, walk, dress and talk. You're being judged at all times. Always overdress slightly. Be clean, smart and a little edgy with what you wear. When you walk through the office, have a slight spring in your step and for gosh sakes stand upright! Look people in the eye. Learn to speak correctly. If you have a regional accent, try to at least soften it.

In the UK, people are especially guilty of making judgments based on the way someone speaks, but even on this side of the pond, it pays to have good speaking skills. My wife and I saw living proof of this when we met *Good Morning America* host Robin Roberts. This former basketball whiz is an amazing woman, and one of the most revered people on national television. Ms. Roberts told us of how her mother made her enunciate clearly and pronounce every word correctly. She wouldn't tolerate lazy sentence structure or poorly articulated words. You can be 100 percent certain that this early training is a solid part of the reason *Good Morning America* has won three consecutive Emmy Awards for Outstanding Morning Program with Robin as anchor.

> COMBAT YOUR
> LIMITING BELIEFS BY
> CONSTANTLY REMINDING
> YOURSELF THAT THEY
> AREN'T TRUE.

In addition to sabotage committed by yourself and your loved ones, several others out there could be intent on destroying your efforts. I'm not being negative; I'm being realistic. There are more sharks out there than you know. We all know the stereotypes of people you should watch out for: stockbrokers, lawyers, mechanics, moneylenders, agents, financial managers and employees who handle your cash. But it is a good idea to be quietly aware of the fact that some people, when presented with the opportunity to rip you off, might do exactly that.

TARGET 11

This is a tough world. Everyone wants some of the pie - your pie. Be alert. If someone offers to make you a fortune, to look after your money, asks for cash up front for some venture, invites you to get involved with pyramid selling, requests your bank and account details, tells you they are incredibly wealthy and can help you or asks for your social insurance number - simply say, "No thanks," and walk away. Don't get drawn back into conversation when they throw another question at you like, "So, you're not interested in making a lot more money than you are earning right now?"

Your answer (the very last time you speak) has to be, "I have absolutely no interest in what you are offering!" Do not give their pitch any further consideration.

AIM FOR THE BULL

- Write down any beliefs that you feel may affect your passion to do well. Remind yourself on a daily basis of why they are not true.

- Be alert. There are more sharks out there than you know.

TARGET 12

Become Obsessed

The world is made up of ordinary people who do extraordinary things. I've been told that I have a great life because I love what I do and have made a good living doing it. But I am well aware that I'm not above average. I'm very ordinary – a guy with the same fears and doubts as others – however, I did get busy with my life. I wanted more and I went for it.

I believe that every person can be a genius at something. It is your responsibility to make yourself aware of this consummate genius and make use of it to reach your full potential. Those who don't succeed have never realized their true abilities.

An important step to finding your inner genius is to realize that your past does not have to define who you are. Dr. Wayne Dyer, in his fantastic book *Excuses Begone!* (Hay House), suggests that the analogy of a speedboat traveling across a lake can be applied to your own life. The wake behind the boat is your past drifting away to nothingness as the boat speeds forward. It doesn't drive the boat – the engine does. When the engine stops, the boat slows and eventually drifts aimlessly, but while the engine is full

TARGET 12

throttle and the boat is headed in the right direction, it gets to its destination in the quickest possible way.

To keep the engine analogy going, it's worth noting that there is ample evidence that many of us are barely getting our motors out of first gear. Our brains have boundless capacities, but these are seldom utilized. Glenn Clark, author of *The Man Who Tapped the Secrets of the Universe,* wrote, "I believe sincerely that every man has consummate genius within him." Obviously some of us are more aware of this magical possession than others. Successful people are those who have discovered this fact for themselves. Those destined for mediocrity, or less, have no positive belief in their innate abilities.

In addition to being a revolutionary retailer, Walmart founder Sam Walton realized the power of positive thinking at an early age. He was a small and not particularly gifted quarterback on the high school football team, but he said his positive attitude was key to helping his team win the state championship. "[The experience] taught me to expect to win, to go into tough challenges always planning to come out victorious," Walton wrote in his autobiography. "It never occurred to me that I might lose; to me, it was almost as if I had a right to win. Thinking like that often seems to turn into a self-fulfilling prophecy."

I recently visited Bentonville, Arkansas, home of Walton's Walmart empire. The purpose of my visit was to meet with

TARGET 12

the Walmart book buyers to try to get their stores to carry my wife Tosca's *Eat-Clean Diet*® book series.

I was told that Bentonville was a small, sleepy town. What a shock I had when I found out that virtually every building was almost brand new. Several hotels had recently been built to accommodate all the manufacturers and wholesalers who travel to Bentonville to meet the Walmart executives responsible for buying products to resell in Walmart's many thousands of stores.

While in Bentonville I visited Sam Walton's original store, saw his 1973 red and white Ford pickup (he found no reason to keep up with the latest models) and spent time staring at his office desk left "as is" since his death in 1992. One piece of paper I picked up contained some of his rules for success. Among the gems of information Sam Walton had written:

- Believe in your business more than anyone else and commit to it.

TARGET 12

- Share your profits with all your associates.
- Day by day strive to motivate your partners. Set high goals and encourage competition.
- Communicate everything to your partners. The more they know, the more they'll understand.
- Tell your associates that you appreciate their good work.
- Show enthusiasm, loosen up and celebrate successes.
- Figure out ways to get your employees to talk, and listen to them.
- Deliver more than you promise. Give customers what they want, and a little more.
- Control your expenses better than your competition. It will give you a competitive advantage.
- Swim upstream. Do what others are not doing. Be daring and unconventional.

So, now I want you to do exactly what the young Sam Walton did during high school. You have to expect to win and you also have to believe, way deep down, that you have a right to win, to succeed and to achieve.

You may want a million dollars in the bank, a slimmer body, a bigger home, an amazing relationship or a superb cottage by a lake. However, wanting these things merely puts you in the category of everybody else. If you want to win, you must see yourself winning, and then give it every ounce of effort to make your prediction come true. This

TARGET 12

will help your subconscious mind realize that you have what it takes. Experts believe that this is a key aspect of positive thinking. Ask an Olympic athlete how he thinks he's going to do in an upcoming event and he'll likely tell you that he's totally psyched to win. Should the thought of losing be in his mind, he's as good as done. No true athlete goes into competition to place second.

When you have a dream, decide for sure that it is truly what you want and then build a picture in your mind of actually owning it. Sometimes collecting photographs or pictures from magazines can help you create a clear and detailed mental image of your success. Once you are able to visualize your desire, you have to take it a step further and emotionalize it as well. What exactly do I mean by this? Assume that as a single guy you have a weight problem you've been unable to beat for years. You want to lose 30 pounds and get a six-pack. But losing weight is only one wish you would like to fulfill.

Your other wish is to go out with that sexy girl in the advertising department – you know, the one you're too shy to approach. Okay! So the answer is clear. You use your desire for this woman to motivate yourself to lose weight by eating clean and exercising regularly. You attach a strong emotion to your goal of getting a six-pack. Once you have made the link and committed to it, you can hardly fail. You can attach emotion to any desire. You just have to look for a way to make a strong connection.

TARGET 12

Edwin C. Barnes is a perfect example of building emotion onto hope. Many moons ago and early on in his life, Barnes had developed a burning desire to work for inven-

> **WHEN YOU ATTACH PASSION TO YOUR DREAM, YOU GET YOURSELF CLOSER TO ACHIEVING IT.**

tor Thomas Edison. Barnes was not well educated. He was poorly dressed and had no money beyond what he spent on traveling by freight train to see Edison. As Barnes made his way to Edison's office he visualized standing before the inventor, telling him that he wanted to be associated with him in his business affairs. He could see himself explaining his strong desire to work with Edison and help him carry out the administrative tasks unrelated to inventing, which was so obviously the sole domain of Edison.

The inventor was so impressed by Barnes' passion and enthusiasm that he gave him a job. Although Barnes was just doing menial office chores for Edison, in is own mind he was already an equal partner of the great inventor.

TARGET 12

Eventually, opportunity presented itself when Barnes noticed that Edison's salesmen were not too keen on selling his strange-looking new dictating machine. Barnes jumped in and persuaded Edison to let him give it a shot. Not surprisingly, Barnes did such an impressive job that Edison gave him a contract to sell the machines across the country. Barnes' burning ambition was realized. The dominating dream of his life had become a reality.

When you attach passion to your dream, you get yourself closer to achieving it. Add emotion and the wish becomes a burning desire. This sparks action and eventually leads to ultimate success.

Elvis Presley, a phenomenon of the '50s, '60s and beyond, built up his passion and powers of visualization by reading comic books. As a child he was a dreamer and as he read, he saw himself as the hero. When he went to the movies on Saturday afternoons to see *Roy Rogers* or *Superman,* he was the fearless cowboy riding Trigger, or Superman himself flying across the skies. Although some might simply view him as a child with an active imagination, I believe that these little fantasies helped supercharge Elvis' efforts to become the world's most famous musician.

Should you find it difficult to partner emotion with your wishes, I suggest you write down your main desire and read it to yourself once in the morning when you wake

TARGET 12

up and once at night before going to bed. As you read, see and feel yourself as having already achieved your goal. Take some time to imagine all of the potential emotions, sights, smells and surroundings – the more details the better!

You may think it impossible to imagine yourself already in possession of a million dollars or more, but here's where burning desire comes into play. You have to turn your mind onto the single objective of wanting, needing and yearning for money. Become obsessed.

My friend John Cardillo, who owned a chain of Canadian gyms called Premier Fitness (interview on page 262), came from a relatively poor family living in Ontario. Most days after school John was required to shop for groceries for his mother and carry the heavy bags back from the store to his home, a distance of just over one mile. John helped out his mother in this way for more than four years, making at least 250 trips each year.

During these arduous and agonizing walks, John would see a string of other people doing their grocery shopping with cars, often Jaguars, Mercedes, BMWs, and sometimes even Rolls Royces and Bentleys. As the days and weeks rolled into months and years, the message became crystal clear. John promised himself that when he grew up, he would never have to carry groceries again. More than that, he vowed he would have sufficient money to do anything he wished.

TARGET 12

This desire burned itself into his head with such certainty and resolve that it drove John to acquire his first gym at the age of 19 and then go on to build one of the largest gym chains in North America.

> IT'S AMAZING
> WHAT HAPPENS
> WHEN YOU LOVE
> WHAT YOU DO. YOUR
> PRODUCTIVITY TRIPLES.

"The secret of success," said Benjamin Disraeli, "is constant purpose." Those who are truly enlightened know what they want out of life and follow the trail with unbridled passion. It's amazing what happens when you love what you do. Your productivity triples. Your energy level is contagious and gets everyone around you excited. Before you know it, everyone's work becomes supercharged with an extra dose of creativity and life.

Remember that there are two kinds of work: Work you have to do and work you want to do. Let's say you're at the end of a long day at the office. You feel tired, listless, drained. You can hardly keep your eyes open, let alone concentrate on the problem at hand. All of a sudden a friend bursts in. "Ready to go play a few holes on the golf course?" or "Wanna go to the ball game?" Wow! Your energy level jumps. Your eyes open wide; a smile breaks across your face. You are totally pumped and ready to go. Because you are interested in playing golf or in watching the game, your energy has skyrocketed. Your interest and mental focus give you energy. You need to have this same interest and passion for your goal.

Passion for what we do is magic. I want you to reclaim that enthusiasm of youth. Wake up every morning full of energy and longing to get at the day. Breathe the fire of passion into everything you do. The more you love your work the happier your weekdays will be.

When I was a teacher, even though I enjoyed the job, I would be somewhat relieved when Friday came along. Today I am so happy with my life that Mondays are no different from Saturdays and Sundays. It's all the same. For

> ## CHOOSE A JOB THAT YOU LOVE AND YOU'LL NEVER HAVE TO WORK A DAY IN YOUR LIFE.
> *- Confucius*

example, writing and planning this book is a delight. As Confucius said, "Choose a job that you love and you'll never have to work a day in your life."

Nothing is impossible for you. Turn on your enthusiasm today. Now! Remember the phrase: "I am the master of my fate; I am the captain of my soul." Henley should have added: "because I have power to control my thoughts." Napoleon Hill reminds us time and time again in his writings: "We have control over but one thing in life: our thoughts."

Riches are not beyond your reach. You can still be what you wish to be. Money, fame, respect, recognition, peace and happiness can be had by all who are ready to develop that burning desire. Lord Byron said it best: "Passion is the element in which we live; without it, we hardly vegetate." There's no doubt that when your desire is strong enough, you will seem to possess the powers of Superman. You have no limits. It's totally up to you. Boy! When I reread this last paragraph I feel my own level of passion flooding my brain, increasing at the very thought of going the extra mile and creating even greater success. Go figure!

TARGET 12

AIM FOR THE BULL

- Let go of the past and start realizing your true capabilities.

- Expect to win.

- Write down what you want. Review it in the morning and before bed. See and feel yourself as having already achieved your goal.

- Attach emotion to your desires. Figure out what you want from life and follow the trail with unbridled passion.

TARGET 13

Do Heed These Don'ts

You've probably heard the saying, "A word to the wise is infuriating," but even so, I am going to give you some advice, some of which I had to learn the hard way – by screwing up.

Now, I'm fully aware that telling people to avoid certain situations, take care and beware of making mistakes is next to useless, but (luckily for you) I'm going to do it anyway. In my time, I wasn't the best at accepting advice. Today, however, if I want to know something I have no problem asking others, especially if those individuals are experts in the field in question.

Many things can cause your plans or your business ventures to fail. It is far better to prevent trouble than to try to treat it after it has occurred. Following are a few don'ts to help prepare you for what you might come up against as you plough your way forward in life.

Don't be Controlled by Negative Thoughts
It may seem a bit insincere to start a list of don'ts with this one, but it's important. Don't let the naysayers (including those in your head) influence your thinking. It's common to have negative thoughts about success. Many people feel

it is actually bad to be successful and, as for having money enough to do the things you want in life, well, that is most definitely an invitation to burn in hell.

Negative thinking is a killer. Often we aren't even aware of how many negative thoughts are racing through our heads at any given moment. Make yourself aware of them and turn them into positive thoughts and images. Remember: Any success you have will be justly earned. It won't come to you without effort. It will come only from your positive planning and careful execution. Expect positive results and that's exactly what you will get.

> AN ENEMY CAN
> SPEND HOURS EACH
> WEEK TRYING TO
> DESTROY YOU AND
> EVERYTHING YOU
> ARE INVOLVED IN.

Don't Fall into the Trap of Smoking and Drinking
Okay, so an occasional drink is acceptable – and I do mean occasional. Alcohol muddies your thinking, saps your energy and is not conducive to success. Smoking, however, is never acceptable. I don't care if your grandfather smoked all his life and lived to 95. If he hadn't smoked at all, he

would have been healthier and fitter, and probably would have lived to 105!

If you smoke now, stop. No ifs, ands or buts. No excuses. You have to stop. Cigarettes are full of poisons. It's true; they are utterly *crammed* with poisons. If I were making this up the cigarette companies would sue me!

When you inhale this lethal poison we call cigarette smoke, it goes from your lungs into your bloodstream, where it is carried to every cell in the body. Think lung cancer is a smoker's only worry? Not on your life. Smokers come down with a huge variety of problems including high blood pressure, heart and circulatory conditions, organ damage – you name it. Quit today. Conquer your bad habits or they will conquer you.

Don't Make Enemies

On the contrary, you should make friends and show those friends your appreciation for all they do.

If you are currently managing or employing people, let them know that you have high regard for their work. The main reason people quit their jobs is because they don't feel appreciated. As a publisher, I have noticed this time and time again. Accordingly, I like to keep my employees informed so they feel they are an integral part of my business, have job security and can, if they work hard, enjoy opportunities and promotions.

TARGET 13

It may at times seem natural to make enemies with someone you don't like or have issues with; however, an enemy can spend hours every week trying to destroy you and everything you are involved in. Remember the golden rule: Do unto others as you would have them do unto you. Become a thoughtful, caring person. Offer help. Be nice.

Don't Be a Letdown

Although there are many people out there who firmly believe in the "under promise and over deliver" business philosophy, there are thousands of people who do the exact opposite. They are letdowns. Always keep your word. It's far better to under promise and over deliver than over promise and under deliver. Keep to your agreements, whether those agreements are million-dollar handshake contracts or promising your wife you'll be home on time. Not keeping to your word sets a dangerous precedent. In time you will be known as untrustworthy and ultimately a liar.

Don't Stop Until It's Done

Do you know people who throw down their pen or close their computers as soon as the clock says 4:30 p.m.? Never mind that their work is unfinished. Ever had a plumber or electrician leave a job before it was done? You may have thought, 'If he had just stayed a half-hour longer I would be able to use my washroom right now.' Arrange your time so that you leave every job well done. Stick it out. Finish something. There is satisfaction in completing a job. This is one of the laws of life.

TARGET 13

Don't Neglect Expert Advice

Henry Ford was called out in a newspaper article as an excessively ignorant man, a person of low intelligence and poor education. The newspaper had a wide circulation and Mr. Ford wasn't too happy.

The case went to court for defamation of character. On the stand, Ford was questioned on his general knowledge of various topics in order to prove his lack of education. Finally he stood up and addressed the judge.

The exact words escape me, but it went something like this: "Your honor, I may not know the name of Henry VIII's third wife, the details of the Crimean War or even the exact weight of the Ford Edsel, but I have employees in place who can give me all the answers I need. I have arranged my business in such a way that I never lack for knowledge on any subject." With that the judge closed the case in favor of Henry Ford. Ford had driven his point home in no uncertain terms.

Don't be a Drifter

The drifter doesn't devote a second to whether he is positive or negative with his thinking. Life controls him, not the other way around. His spare time is spent with his television set, computer and video games. He allows his mind to be filled with any stray thoughts that come along. The drifter has no regard for time and cares little about anything positive in nature.

TARGET 13

The non-drifter has certainty to his thoughts. He is determined, positive and passionate about everything in life that can improve him and make him a more useful human being.

Don't Close Your Eyes to the World

James Watt's fascination with the powerful steam coming out of his mother's kettle led him to eventually improve the efficiency of the steam engine, which allowed it to power the Industrial Revolution. Speaking of revolutions, 13-year-old Bill Gates was entranced by his school's only computer, spending all of his spare time writing programs for it (and I think we all know how that story ends).

Open your eyes wide and drink in the miracles of the world that surrounds you. When you have learned to see, then you can learn to think, and ultimately put the two together.

Don't be Careless with Words

Words, whether written or spoken, put out certain energy to others. The saying "sticks and stones may break my bones, but words will never hurt me" is utter nonsense. Words can damage a person's entire psyche. Words can ruin relationships in one sentence. Words can ruin careers. They can even take down whole companies or countries. Beware of what you say to others. Idle gossip may be fun at times but it can get you into deep trouble. You may make people happy and content or put them into a state of excessive depression and damage them for the rest of their life. Try to edit what you say before your mouth forms the words. Speak only after consideration. As Swiss poet Johann K. Lavater said, "Never tell evil of a man, if you do not know it for a certainty, and if you know it for a certainty, then ask yourself, 'Why should I tell it?'"

AIM FOR THE BULL

- Banish all negative thoughts. Expect success and that's what you'll get.

- Conquer your bad habits or they will conquer you.

- Be nice. (I know it sounds academic, but give it a try.)

- Don't be a letdown.

- Stick it out – finish every job.

- Open your eyes and find something to become passionate about.

- Watch what you say to others.

TARGET 14

Kick Negativity to the Curb and Stomp On It

Master statesman Winston Churchill is quoted as saying, "A pessimist sees the difficulty in every opportunity; an optimist sees the opportunity in every difficulty." We all have a certain degree of negativity. It's that spineless voice that feeds doubts to our thoughts. If you want to give importance to improving yourself, you must do all you can to keep negativity at bay. As with any other skill, the courage to think positively can be learned and ultimately acquired. We all have acquaintances who grumble and complain about everything in sight. It's not always practical to consign them to the trash pile; however, we do not have to let their negativity rub off on us. This can take some effort. My own approach is to concentrate on not doing, seeing, smelling, thinking, hearing or feeling anything I don't wish to do, see, smell, think, hear or feel. When I come across racist talk, unsubstantiated gossip, criticism and badmouthing of others, I invariably turn the other way and avoid the situation.

Pay attention only to what you want to do, think, see and hear. Don't surround yourself with negative-thinking people. We humans have a strong tendency to take on the

TARGET 14

characteristics of the people we surround ourselves with. Are you currently locked into a job that screams of negativity? Are you fearful of getting out of a negative relationship? Do you fear changing certain "set" habits like tobacco and alcohol, or even prescription drugs? These things are mental monsters that have settled into your consciousness. Muster every ounce of your resolve to beat these gremlins. You can do it. And when victory is yours, you will thank yourself over and over for having the courage to beat the odds.

> ## GIVE YOURSELF THE GIFT OF ONGOING POSITIVE FOCUS.

When things are going well for us, we tend to stick to positive thoughts. However, what happens when things turn sour? (I know it seems negative to assume this will happen, but as Longfellow wrote, "Into each life some rain must fall.") We need to learn the skill of seeing the best in every situation because without optimism we develop a feeling of hopelessness, one of the most overwhelming emotions in the world.

Give yourself the gift of ongoing positive focus. It must be worked for, developed and nurtured in your head. If you are going to be successful, you must lose the habit of using

TARGET 14

phrases like "I can't do it," "It's too hard," "It's beyond my ability," "I wish I had" and "If only."

Negative phrases such as these, used frequently enough, will disempower you. They will sap you of your physical and mental fortitude. How are you ever going to achieve maximum health, strength of character, enthusiasm, passion, wealth and a profusion of joy without the positive attitude needed? You must stay in a state of mind where you see yourself as a success only. You will achieve good results with a strong commitment to the job at hand.

> ## PAY ANY PRICE TO STAY IN THE PRESENCE OF EXTRAORDINARY PEOPLE.
> *- Mike Murdock*

Negativity in the workplace can be especially sinister. In fact, the attitude of one negative employee can actively permeate and destroy the attitude of all the others. The opposite effect can also occur from one who is a positive thinker. Good vibes may be similarly spread among fellow workers.

In *The Success Principles* (Harper Collins), Jack Canfield dug up a marvelous quote by Mike Murdock, author of

TARGET 14

The Leadership Secrets of Jesus: "Pay any price to stay in the presence of extraordinary people." I love it. I have been in the presence of a few extraordinary people and I have most definitely learned something valuable from each and every one of them! Although I have seen both Picasso and Brigitte Bardot in person, I have not had a chance to really be in their presence. Sadly, it is too late for me to meet the artist, but I would love to one day meet the French bombshell, as I write this, now well into her 70s.

I'm sure you've met negative people who just can't get interested in life and all the opportunities that are presented on a daily basis. Teenagers in particular are susceptible to a dose of negativity, causing them to roll their eyes at the slightest suggestion that they do something useful instead of going on Facebook, lazing on the couch watching TV, text messaging the whole world and hanging out and partying. Not to mention the strange need for only five hours of sleep a night, junk food, booze and even experimentation with so-called recreational drugs.

Take this very moment to stamp out that negative voice in your head that says, "What's the use?" Instead, search your mind for something of interest, a passion you can get excited about. Each of us is transported to Earth with a purpose. We need to recognize this and not get sidetracked by mundane matters as we make our way through life. "It's so easy to be a drifter," says Napoleon

TARGET 14

Hill, "and accomplish nothing of worth. But with purpose everything falls into place."

In his book *Unstoppable Confidence* (McGraw-Hill), Kent Sayre says, "Ask yourself, if money were no object and you knew you could not fail, what would you do in your life? The immediate answer to this question is your passion. It is what you should do with your life." Once you've got the answer, you've got to apply action according to the philosophy of this book – massive action that will drown out all negativity knocking at your front door.

At the conclusion of each day, preferably right before you turn in for the night, it's a good idea to plan the next day's adventures and also engage in a bit of reflection. When you do this, your subconscious mind digests your thoughts, processes them and places them in sequence. Sometimes you may find that you wake up with ideas that rekindle your inspiration, excite you and help you build a stronger creative mindset, which, in turn, will continue to help you succeed. Make sure to keep pen and paper by your bed to record these thoughts as they occur – otherwise you may find them lost forever in the light of day.

I am a believer in writing things down. I carry around a single piece of paper and a pen everywhere I go. When I see or hear something of interest, I make a note of it and eventually transcribe the really good ideas into a big notebook. I'm also an ardent collector of images torn from

TARGET 14

magazines, books and newspapers. It's a good idea to always have pencil and paper, digital recorder, cell phone or tablet handy at all times to record inspiring notes, images and audio files.

> ## FINDING TIME IS
> ## AN ART.

One often-used phrase by negative people is "I don't have time." The truth is, not one person on this planet has more hours in his day than anyone else. Finding time is an art. We should not spend hours on meaningless, unimportant things at the expense of more urgent matters. Just being a more responsible TV viewer or Internet user can gain the average person three or four hours a day. Food for thought.

The more negativity you kill off, the better your chances of totally achieving your dreams. Napoleon Hill writes in *Think and Grow Rich*, "Positive and negative emotions cannot occupy the mind at the same time. One or the other must dominate. It is your responsibility to make sure positive emotions constitute the dominating influence of your mind."

The world is yours. It's time to grab it with both hands and shout, "Eureka! I'm on my way."

AIM FOR THE BULL

- Learn the skill of seeing the best in every situation.

- Surround yourself with positive people.

- Stamp out the negative voices and, instead, search your mind for a passion you can get excited about.

- Organize your thoughts by engaging in a bit of reflection before bed.

- Record ideas the moment they come to mind before they are lost during your day's busy activities.

TARGET 15

Maintain Important Relationships

One of the most potent pieces of advice I can give you is that no matter what you have achieved, no matter how many Ferraris sit in your driveway, the quality and enjoyment you get from life comes down to your health and relationships. Don't neglect your home life.

All too often we drift through family life without taking time to maintain the closeness that keeps us tight knit and happy. We communicate but do not connect, or at least we do not preserve our connections as we could or should. The most important thing of all is to share your thoughts with your spouse and children. Let them in on your work aspirations. Get to know theirs. Ask their opinions. Time spent nourishing your relationships is time well spent. As Stephen Covey says, "You always reap what you sow; there is no shortcut."

In addition, you will feel truly content with your existence only if you have been of service to your fellow man. Realize that we come into this beautiful world with nothing, and we are destined to leave with nothing. But while on Earth we can make a difference, however small, by contributing to others' lives in meaningful ways.

TARGET 15

I'm not saying you shouldn't be concerned with making a living or striving to be wealthy. I'm merely asking you to imbue your actions with a sense of justice and fairness. Compassion and daily acts of kindness make life far richer and more rewarding. Take time each morning to think about how you can inject both your work and home life with deeds of kindness and consideration.

> ## COMMUNICATION IS KEY TO A HEALTHY AND HAPPY HOME LIFE.

Communication is key to a healthy and happy home life. Take time for conversation and relationship building in the family home. Mealtimes are the perfect opportunity for this. Whenever humanly possible, meals should be enjoyed together as a family. Make it a rule that no electronic devices are allowed at the dinner table and try to foster a fun and relaxed environment in which everyone feels comfortable expressing their feelings without fear of judgment. Voices should never be raised at mealtimes.

One of the first steps to building strong and healthy relationships is to examine what you've learned about them from your experiences with your own family. How were you brought up as a child? Were you practically ignored or

TARGET 15

did you have constant support and love? Maybe one parent gave you the cold shoulder while the other smothered you with love and affection. How did each approach make you feel? Use these memories to help you think about the type of parent you want to be. Every upbringing is different, but examining yours can be a valuable tool in helping you connect with your family members.

Even if you're not a parent, you still need to focus on strengthening relationships with your friends, colleagues, relatives and neighbors – your life depends on it. Seriously. According to a 2010 Brigham Young University study, researchers found that having satisfying social relationships boosts our odds of survival by 50 percent. The researchers also found that having poor social ties is just as harmful to overall health as smoking almost a pack of cigarettes a day. "Our relationships can have direct health benefits," said Julianne Holt-Lunstad, Ph.D., coauthor of the study's report. "They can help us cope with stress. We know we can count on people and have these resources available."

Currently, I have a family of four girls and one amazing wife. My son, Braden, passed away in 2011 as a result of a tragic car accident. He was 23 years old. I cannot stress the importance of keeping in touch with family members enough. When they are gone, they are gone. I think about my dear Braden every day.

TARGET 15

When my father had to be placed in a retirement home at the age of 90, my wife and I would visit him every week and enjoy a friendly get-together. Aware that his life was well into its autumn years, we would ask him questions about his youth, the war and his escape from Europe to Britain in 1938 when Hitler invaded Austria.

One day, after enjoying an afternoon tea and sandwiches, we said our goodbyes and left him sitting at the table. Suddenly, I remembered a question that I had been meaning to ask him for weeks. When the elevator stopped at the lobby, I pressed the button to go back up to my father's floor, but, at that moment, a couple in wheelchairs was entering the elevator. They needed the entire elevator space to get both wheelchairs in at the same time.

In a split second I abandoned my mission to go back up to see my father, telling myself that I would definitely make a point of asking him that question during next week's visit. That night my father died. I never got to ask my question. I implore you to mend bridges and make the most of being with family and friends. Don't leave it too late. You will assuredly regret it if you do.

When I lived in London, I spent several years living with my actor friend, Harry. We shared a lot of good times, including numerous trips to Cannes in the south of France in May, during film festival time.

TARGET 15

OPEN YOUR ARMS
TO LIFE'S JOYS, PASSIONS,
TEARS AND LAUGHTER –
AND THE FAMILY
MEMBERS WHO BRING
THEM ABOUT.

When I moved to North America, we lost touch with each other. I would make halfhearted attempts to reach Harry, but never succeeded. Last year I finally tracked him down and got talking to his 23-year-old daughter, whom I had last seen as a baby.

Finally, I said, "How is your dad? Can you get him on the phone?"

She went silent. "I'm sorry, but dad died two years ago of lung cancer."

What a fool I had been in allowing so much time to pass without making a stronger effort to reconnect with him. I believe that one of our greatest sins is to be moved by nothing; to strive for nothing; to travel through life without appreciating this Earth and the beauty that surrounds us. Open your arms to life's joys, passions, tears and laughter – and the family members who bring them about. Grab life

TARGET 15

by the lapels and pull yourself into positive connection with every opportunity. Get involved. As Albert Einstein said, "Rejoice with your family in the beautiful land of life."

AIM FOR THE BULL

- At the beginning of each day, take some time to think about how you can inject both your work and home life with deeds of kindness and consideration.

- Examine what you've learned about relationships from experiences with your own childhood and use this knowledge to help you become a more compassionate parent.

- Remember that life is short. Mend bridges and make the most of being with family and friends – now!

TARGET 16

Optimize Everything: Take Ideas and Improve on Them

My first ventures into publishing on a large scale were with magazines. After a few years I went into publishing books. It seemed like a natural progression. Besides, I could publicize the books in my magazines and even mention the magazines in the books. A one-hand-washes-the-other kind of thing.

Originally, I concentrated on publishing books on what I knew best – physical fitness. I would purchase a book-length manuscript from one of our magazine freelancers, toss it to one of our artists and tell them to select some photos from our files. I would spend little time reading the manuscripts, even less checking the graphics.

When the book design was finished I would ship it off to the printers. My choice of paper would be based on price and often that meant the book would be printed on spongy, non-glossy paper that made all the photography look weak.

TARGET 16

From the printers, the book went to our distributor and, as for marketing, each book was mentioned a couple of times in our magazines, and *only* a couple of times.

After a few years of underwhelming results a light bulb went on in my head. The word "optimization" came to me one day as I was lining up to pay for groceries at the checkout. Why it occurred at this particular moment, I don't know. In an instant I knew what I had to do.

> ## AFTER A FEW YEARS OF UNDERWHELMING RESULTS, A LIGHT BULB WENT ON IN MY HEAD.

The next manuscript I bought, I read very carefully. I asked the writer for some revisions, and requested an additional chapter. The photo support was carefully vetted and additional images were shot to better fit with the text. I selected our top graphics artist and supervised and checked every layout. I chose a glossy paper for the inside of the book and heavier paper for the cover.

We employed a top-notch new distributor who had a proven record in handling fitness publications. When it came to promotions I contacted radio and TV stations, hired a

TARGET 16

public relations firm and mentioned the book relentlessly in our magazines. I began optimizing *every* aspect of book production, marketing and distribution.

This optimization totally turned around my book sales volume. We went from a book department that was breaking even at best to one that was making a healthy profit each and every month.

Of course we incurred added costs, what with more expensive paper stock, photography and the hiring of a PR firm. However, there was no added cost to putting more plugs in our magazines, better graphic design and obtaining a superior distributor. Conclusion: The additional cost and effort was well worth it. We have sold almost three million books since I adopted my optimization principle as opposed to mere thousands before.

Part of optimization is paying attention to detail. I admit I fall a little short on this one. I wish I were better at detail than I am. If you are young and not set in your ways you could train yourself to be a detail person. Changing your ways can be difficult, like learning to ride a bike or driving a car, but in time your brain and muscles learn how, and things become second nature. Alternatively, should you have the means, you can pay someone else to be the detail person in your life.

TARGET 16

Jack Canfield, co-creator of *Chicken Soup for the Soul*, reminds us that the word *kaizen* is Japanese for constant and never-ending improvement. I love it. Too bad we don't have a single word in the English language with that meaning. Kaizen is an operating philosophy for millions of successful people. My old friend and publishing competitor Joe Weider, founder of *Shape* and *Muscle & Fitness* magazines, was always keeping his eye out for new moneymaking ideas. They seldom came out of his own creative juices, but Joe had his own genius: He would take other people's ideas and improve on them. Nothing wrong with that.

For example, he got the name for his successful bodybuilding publication from a popular shampoo at the time named Flex. The title for his exercise magazine was taken from an already established publication in Australia, *Muscle & Fitness*. He would optimize and frequently turn mundane concepts into huge moneymaking machines. Joe never missed a trick.

When he retired from publishing he talked David Pecker, publisher of the tabloids *Star, National Enquirer* and

> THE WORD *KAIZEN* IS
> JAPANESE FOR CONSTANT
> AND NEVER-ENDING
> IMPROVEMENT.

TARGET 16

Globe, into paying $350 million for his various titles. He also rented out his building to Mr. Pecker and on top of that retained a 10 percent interest in the business itself. Talk about optimization.

Another trick of optimizing your business life is to surround yourself with experts. If you want to learn about carpentry, get yourself in the company of successful carpenters. Want money? Be around people who have a ton of it!

I get people asking me how to get on the cover of one of my magazines, but very few people have enough courage to come up to me and ask about publishing. I know many experts who say the same thing. People seldom ask for advice. Yet most successful people are happy to give out advice when asked, if they have time. Those struggling to make it seldom want to give out anything, but those who have made it to the top are invariably pleased and humbled to give out helpful advice.

To keep yourself on target to improve the various aspects of your business, pick one aspect of your lifestyle or business and ask yourself how you can improve this one thing. Once you have made it better, move on to another. If you fail to optimize you run the risk of going stale and things will deteriorate.

TARGET 16

When we think of a masterpiece like Michelangelo's frescoes on the walls of the Sistine Chapel, we don't just think of the one figure; we think of the entire work, the piece as a whole. I can say the same of the genius of the movie *Avatar,* or an Elton John creation. We don't just think of one aspect, but the complete collection of artistry. Good thinking is similar. Put it all together and you will achieve personal greatness.

Have you noticed that very few people these days go the extra mile? Yet this is a trait of the successful achiever. When you go the extra mile you put yourself in line for exceeding expectations. You've observed it yourself, I'm sure. Remember when someone gave you more than you paid for; more than you expected? That didn't go unnoticed, did it? You, too, can give people more than they expect. It's a form of optimization that will pay off for both of you.

Richard Carlson, Ph.D., in his book *Don't Sweat the Small Stuff About Money* (Hyperion) explained that when his dad read his school essays he said, "Richard, it doesn't matter that you're not a great speller. But it's really important that you know you're not a good speller. That way, when in doubt, you can use a dictionary." In other words, understand what your weaknesses are, so you can get help with them. We can all use the knowledge and experience of others.

TARGET 16

Optimization is simply living by a higher set of standards for everything you do in business and in pleasure. The world will respond with mammoth enthusiasm.

AIM FOR THE BULL

- Part of optimization is paying attention to detail.

- Live by a high set of standards in everything.

- Additional cost in effort pays off.

- Go the extra mile when possible.

TARGET 17

Partner Boldness With Vision and You'll Make a Two-Thumbs-Up Movie of Your Life

The size of your success is measured by the strength of your desire. Be unafraid of attempting larger things. Convince yourself that you are important and that nothing is beyond your reach. Build courage to take responsibility and dare to tread where others have feared to go.

Boldness is important, unaccompanied by rudeness or unmannerly behavior of course. Goethe's wonderful quote contains the most inspiring words ever created: "Whatever you can do or dream, you can begin it. Boldness has genius, power and magic to it."

Boldness is often tied to change, and traditionally the populace in general is very much against change. For the most part, people resent having to make changes in their lifestyle or at their workplace. In his book *Winning* (HarperCollins), Jack Welch told of an incident: "The *Times* of London changed to a tabloid format, and the editor told me he received a letter asking how it felt to be the per-

TARGET 17

son responsible for ending western civilization." However, never before in history has change been so in vogue as it is today. Change is a positively critical part of life, business, and survival. You need to change, and you should do it on your terms before you absolutely have to.

Arnold Schwarzenegger, whom I have known for almost 45 years now, has endured many hardships over his career. He told me: "Struggle is what builds strength, not winning. When you go through hardships and decide not to surrender, that is strength."

> ## WHAT'S THE POINT OF DREAMING ABOUT SOMETHING IF YOU LACK THE BOLDNESS TO PURSUE IT?

Most people lack boldness when it comes to achievement. They are just too timid. "We are as babes in the cradle," said Virginia Woolf. Confidence and the boldness that comes with it matters more than almost anything else in determining your success. Without it you are stuck in a rut. What's the point of dreaming about something if you lack the boldness to pursue it? Shyness, overt modesty and timidity could be described as enemies of success. The very possession of these traits is a wall keeping you from getting what you want out of life.

A large part of my life has been associated with the bodybuilding and fitness world. I have known all the champions and hardly a day goes by that I am not introduced to a new physical fitness personality of some kind.

> ## BOLDNESS DOES NOT HAVE TO BE ARROGANCE. IT IS MERELY BORN OUT OF CONFIDENCE.

Recently, I was introduced to the newest Mr. Universe. He approached me with his arms way out to the side (looking as though he was carrying an invisible roll of carpet under each arm). He appeared completely stiff, awkward and unnatural. When we shook hands, he squeezed so hard I swear he was trying to crush my fingers. From these actions I could tell that he was compensating for his lack of personal confidence.

Contrast this guy with a real physical culture champion like Arnold Schwarzenegger. Arnold doesn't puff out his chest, wear tight tank tops or try to break fingers when he gives a handshake. Invariably, he wears a long-sleeve shirt, jacket and tie. He doesn't have to boast about his history-making seven Mr. Olympia wins or his numerous Mr. Universe titles. One can see by his general appearance that he keeps himself fit, shapely and free of excess weight. Unlike many overdeveloped bodybuilders, Arnold exudes confidence without the need to suck in his waist, expand his chest and spread his latissimus dorsi.

Boldness does not have to be arrogance. It is merely born out of confidence. Men and women with bold vision and confidence do not have to preen or talk aggressively to push their existence down our throats. A bold person is optimistic. No successful leader was ever a pessimist. Presidents Franklin D. Roosevelt and Ronald Reagan both came to power in their respective days and boldly pushed a new spirit of hope into America when the country needed it most. This world needs more people like them. In fact every activity needs a strong character willing to boldly lead the way. Every business, every home, every city, every country urgently needs leaders of integrity and fortitude.

Never let others influence your choice to lead or to determine whether you can or cannot accomplish a certain task. If a project is important to you, own it! And boldly follow your passion. Men and women with the courage to act with unabashed vision while others cower behind a veil of fear, will become dominant. Boldness partnered with vision will make a two-thumbs-up movie of your life.

TARGET 17

Boldness works when your customers are bold in their praise for you and your product. You have to deliver great service or a great product, so amazing that your customers don't just like it; they absolutely love it. Set your standards so high that your customers will rave about what you are delivering. In this way your product or service will soar in popularity. It will go viral.

> WE SHOULD NOT LET OUR FEARS HOLD US BACK FROM PURSUING OUR HOPES.
>
> *- John F. Kennedy*

Don't be afraid to boldly ask for what you want. The results will astonish you. Few people will dare to ask for something they want because they consider it may be rude or, worse, they may get rejected. Have no fear. Ask in the right way and neither will be the case.

Additionally, learn to ask questions. Ask for answers from those who you feel know more than you do. Ask why. If you want to put some big shot on the spot, especially if he makes a statement that doesn't seem to make sense or appears downright impossible, ask that very searching and feared question: "How do you know?"

TARGET 17

John F. Kennedy put it all in context: "We should not let our fears hold us back from pursuing our hopes."

AIM FOR THE BULL

- Being bold in business is rewarding.

- Boldness doesn't mean you are arrogant.

- Do not hesitate to ask for what you want.

- No successful leader was ever a pessimist.

TARGET 18

Prepare Yourself
for a Downturn

I don't know one established business that hasn't experienced a serious downturn. It can happen. It will happen. Many of you reading this will have experienced a downturn in your business activities already. Maybe it was the economy, or perhaps it was a competitive business that rose out of nowhere to challenge your bottom line. Whatever the reason, downturns are inevitable and to be successful you have to be prepared for survival.

These days businesses might be fined by government agencies because of labeling laws, false advertising, ingredient claims, unhygienic work conditions or one of many other reasons – the list is endless. Sometimes the problems can be catastrophic, as with the Toyota recall of millions of cars, mad cow disease affecting beef sales or the salmonella problem involving a billion eggs. You may encounter tax problems at some point. No one likes paying tax. Your accountant should see to it that you pay the very least possible, legally. Paying more than you should is madness, but you do have to pay according to the current rules of law and tax avoidance can certainly come back to haunt you. Threats can seem to come out of thin air. If you are working for a company, trouble could come your way from vindictive colleagues, snippy bosses or decisions from the top regarding downsizing, new technology, systems changes, saving money and so on.

When things seem really bad and you feel like throwing in the towel – don't! You may be just a few inches from success. One of the most common causes of failure is the habit of giving up in the face of what appears to be total defeat. We have all been guilty of this habit at one time or another. To illustrate, here's a true story that took place about 100 years ago in Colorado.

Robert Darby, a very successful insurance broker, told the story of his uncle, who had been totally infatuated with the thought of discovering gold. He had gold fever and set off in the gold rush days to make his fortune. He staked a claim and went to work, manually hauling rocks and dirt with a pick and shovel.

> ## WHEN THINGS SEEM REALLY BAD AND YOU FEEL LIKE THROWING IN THE TOWEL – DON'T!

TARGET 18

> VERY FEW PEOPLE
> ARE ABLE TO FACE
> ADVERSITY AND TURN IT
> INTO OPPORTUNITY. YOU
> CAN BE ONE WHO BEATS
> THE ODDS.

As luck would have it, his hard work paid off when he discovered gold. To excavate the shining ore efficiently he needed machinery, so he rushed back to his neighborhood in Maryland, telling his relatives and a few neighbors of the strike. They all chipped in, bought the required machinery and had it shipped to the mine head.

Robert Darby and his uncle went to work in the mine. The returns showed that they had one of the richest mines in Colorado. The mined gold paid off various debts and a huge profit was in the cards.

Then, suddenly, the vein of gold ore disappeared. The gravy train ground to a halt. They could locate no more gold. They drilled on desperately, hoping to hit more of the precious metal, but to no avail. Ultimately, they decided to give up.

The uncle sold the machinery to a junk dealer for a few hundred dollars and made his way back to Maryland. Some junk men are a bit slow, but not this one. He called in a mining engineer to check out the mine. The engineer concluded that the vein of ore had been broken because of a fault line. He suggested that drilling a mere three feet farther from where the Darbys had stopped drilling could pick up the vein again. The junk dealer took hundreds of millions of dollars from the mine because he had consulted an expert before giving up.

As for Darby, he learned his lesson and would often tell of his folly. He would frequently tell friends that he "stopped three feet from gold" and that he would never again give up on a project without being assured that he was 100 percent correct. He went on to become a successful entrepreneur after learning to never quit on anything too soon.

Each of us faces problems at some time in our life. No one is immune. It is how you react to these problems that makes the difference. This is what sets you apart, brings success when others fail and ultimately determines what you become and what you accomplish. It's how you decide to fight the negativity of these obstacles that makes or breaks your path to success. Very few people are able to face adversity and turn it into opportunity. You can be one who beats the odds.

Remember the old story of the two identical twins? One guy was a drunk and had a horrendously poor quality of life. The other fellow was hugely successful and healthy.

A reporter asked the drunk what he blamed his condition on. The reply, "My father was a drunk. What chance did I have?" The reporter then asked the successful twin what he felt his success was due to. He answered, "My father was a drunk. I vowed I wouldn't be like him."

How many times have you heard the story of people crying because they lost their job, got laid off or just couldn't take the pressure at work? It happens. Maybe it's happened to you. Sometimes it may seem as if your whole world is crumbling around you. Sometimes people even attempt suicide when afflicted by the misfortunes of personal circumstances. However, frequently the survivors of these attempts say on recovery, "What was I thinking? Life is great. I'm so glad to be alive." Problems are seldom as bad as they seem at the time. When you come to a roadblock in life, take a detour. It may take both time and work, but persevere until you find a solution. Never give up. Difficulties are frequently, if not always, opportunities to achieve higher objectives.

Setbacks come to us all. They will come to you. We just have to know how to deal with them. Setbacks, though it may be hard to believe when we are actually experiencing them, help us grow and move to a higher place. And unbelievably, when they have faded away into the past, those

TARGET 18

most affected often declare they are happy to have experienced their own setback. "I'm glad I lost my job, because it paved the way for me to be here," is something we hear on a regular basis.

> ## WHEN YOU COME TO
> ## A ROADBLOCK IN LIFE,
> ## TAKE A DETOUR.

Going bankrupt these days is a very strong reality. Many people bought houses in the early part of this century with no money down. Their monthly payments were high, and when the economic downturn raised its ugly head and unemployment hit the masses, the owners often found making payments with any type of regularity to be nearly impossible. A sad state of affairs, yes. If you are ever in this state, however, think of everything you can do to turn things around before you go bankrupt. Be creative.

I don't want to end this chapter on a poor note. My simple request is that when a downturn comes, address it with common sense and creative thinking about the opportunities that are presented to you. You may not see them at first, but they are there.

AIM FOR THE BULL

- You have to be ready for a downturn.

- Don't automatically give up when things go bad.

- Address a downturn with creative common sense.

- Setbacks can help us grow and move to a higher place.

TARGET 19

Project Your Personality By Being Attractive, Sincere and Agreeable

When discussing attractiveness, let's not give even one second of thought to the way our DNA caused our features to turn out. Attractiveness is not based on the structure of your face. Attractiveness comes from your demeanor, your smile, the energy in your eyes. We are, after the age of 30, responsible for our own facial appearance. Added to that is the way we speak, stand, sit, walk, shake hands and behave in the company of others.

Cleanliness is paramount. We simply can't be too clean or too groomed. Our clothing has to be immaculate, tinged with adventure, our teeth clean and in good repair, our hair styled and washed, and even our nose hairs have to be trimmed on a regular basis. (My wife keeps reminding me about this. I know, too much information.)

You will have noticed, I'm sure, that many facially attractive men and women turn out to be less than interesting as you get to know them. Some have such lousy personalities

TARGET 19

> ## THE SUN IS OUT, YOU'RE AS HEALTHY AS A HORSE AND, A MILLION PRAISES TO OUR CREATOR, YOU ARE AT THIS MOMENT ABOVE GROUND!

that they could be perceived, after being around them for a couple of hours, as being downright ugly.

However, when you get even a poorly structured face that projects a smile with twinkling eyes that light up a room with their energy – well, that person is undeniably attractive. As Richard Templar says in *The Rules of Work* (Prentice Hall), "Smiles that light up a room are magnetic and powerful; eyes that twinkle and are full of life are enough to make us think the whole face is good looking." And needless to say, an air of confidence (not cockiness) is extremely attractive. There's a difference between being confident and being cocky. The former will bring you admirers while the latter will make you more enemies than you could imagine in your worst nightmare.

I don't need to go into every detail of grooming etiquette, do I? You know the importance of daily showering, hair

TARGET 19

grooming, nail trimming, shaving, plus having clean hands free of food remains, oil, soil and nicotine stains.

Women are masters at assessing strangers with a one-second glance. They take it all in just like that. Women are especially adept at knowing every aspect of your personality by a single glance at ... wait for it ... your shoes! For gosh sakes keep them clean and in good repair, otherwise you are doomed.

Okay, I'll admit some people can get away with looking scruffy, but they usually have excessive good looks or else they are scintillating personalities in their own right.

An attractive personality incorporates so many things, not the least of which is our attitude toward others and the world at large. Don't be a whiner or a moaner, and don't complain about life, at least not habitually. Complaining identifies you as petty and trivial, and can give others the impression that you are negative through and through. It will take the place of positive thoughts and actions that could well put you on the road to a far more fulfilled life. Besides, people just won't want to be around you. Remember, if it really isn't a horrendously bad day (and yes, they do come along from time to time), it is a good day. And you'd better believe it's a good day. The sun is in the sky, you're as healthy as a horse and, a million praises to our creator, you are at this moment above ground!

TARGET 19

Sincerity is key to gaining people's trust. Nobody likes a person who oozes insincerity. You can get away with lacking knowledge or know-how, but when others come to realize that there is no substance or sincerity to your character, then your aspirations for a successful, fulfilled life are in jeopardy. Being insincere today may have roots in your early upbringing. Make an attempt to care about what others say and do. Care about the world at large. Be sincere.

Build friendships whenever possible. A true friend can give sincere advice and opinions that others dare not render. You may find you can be closer and more honest with your best friend than your wife, children or even your mother. Friends respect each other in spite of circumstances that might point toward the contrary.

Develop your personal habits to the extent that you can work, eat, drink and socialize in any company. Be polite to store clerks and waiters. Show courtesy to all who you deal with. Be at your best always. Have good manners. This does not mean that you have to cock your little finger while partaking in your afternoon Earl Grey tea. It does, however, imply that you should not pick up your dinner bowl and noisily slurp down the remains of your cream of potato soup.

How we treat others is important. The basic rule here is to treat others as we would wish to be treated. Talking too much and listening too little is a fault shared by 90 percent of us. Far better that you tactfully draw people into conversation. Be genuinely interested in what's going on in their lives. By keeping your ears open and your mouth shut you will learn far more than others who choose to blab nonstop with unguarded enthusiasm. To listen is to learn; make sure you assimilate what you learn. Much of it will serve you well in the future.

> HOW WE TREAT OTHERS
> IS IMPORTANT. THE BASIC
> RULE HERE IS TO TREAT
> OTHERS AS WE WOULD
> WISH TO BE TREATED.

Always involve yourself in acceptable behavior. Never lose your temper. Refuse to drink alcohol to any point at which you begin to lose control. Be responsible. Think before you speak. How many times have you blurted out something that almost immediately you wish you hadn't verbalized? Editing your conversation that split-second before your mouth throws out the words can save you a lot of hassles. A similar control should be placed on your answers when asked for an opinion. Does the questioner really want to know the truth, half the truth, or just a noncommittal answer? The wrong words out of your mouth can crucify an impressionable personality. One should never lie, but there are occasions when holding back on the entire truth may be beneficial both to a relationship and the receiver's peace of mind.

Every aspect of your personality in addition to your manner of dress and grooming speak for or against your confidence. Accordingly, if you are employed as a non-manager yet want to be promoted to a managerial position, you should observe how the current successful managers conduct themselves; how they dress, walk, talk and generally administer and control their day. Without making a sudden transformation, which would appear strange, you should gradually slide into any planned metamorphosis. Nothing makes a person feel more uncomfortable than being seriously under- or overdressed, and suddenly prancing about the office in a way that is totally foreign to your normal behavior will bring you more raised eyebrows than a troop of trumpet players suddenly turning up in your bedroom.

Promptness is extremely important. Your friends and associates will come to rely on you. Turn up when you say you will. Be reliable. Be on time at your desk each day. The boss will notice, believe me. Time is running a race with every human being. Be on time and don't waste the precious minutes and hours of others. Don't be a letdown.

When I was attending Culford School just outside Bury St. Edmunds in the UK during my teens, my parents would occasionally arrange to meet outside Palmer's restaurant after spending an hour or so looking around the town's shops. My father, mother and I would each go our separate ways and arrange to meet at 5 o'clock on the dot. It was always "on the dot." The only trouble was, my father and I would be on time but my mother, bless her, just couldn't manage it. On some occasions she kept us waiting for almost an hour.

This never really changed until one day my father, normally a patient man, suddenly burst forward with: "There's nothing worse than a letdown!" I can remember this exclamation of frustration as though it were yesterday.

AIM FOR THE BULL

- It's attractive to be neat and clean.

- Letting people down is not a good point.

- Complaining makes one unattractive.

TARGET 20

When You Find a Mentor You Get the Feeling: If He Can Do It, I Can Do It

As I mentioned in Target 1, I was lucky enough to know the richest man in the world, a Texan, Jean Paul Getty. I was in my 20s at the time, and our mutual interest in body-building and weightlifting brought us together. I first met him at the annual NABBA Mr. Universe contest held at the London Palladium Theatre, Drury Lane. In truth we didn't talk business because it would have been ridiculous for me as a teacher of art and a mere fan of lifting weights to discuss business operations with the world's richest man. But talk we did, about almost everything else. Above all, as is often the case when in the company of famous people, I remembered virtually everything he said. Also, much of what I learned came from observation. I loved his home, Sutton Place, a grand estate in the country with a long winding private entrance, crossing a stream and then suddenly the elegant mansion, in front of which was an entire field of daffodils.

Getty gave me confidence. Because of our friendship I felt I could go into business for myself and do well. As it turned out we also had a mutual love of art. At the time Getty was planning to build an Italian-style museum in Malibu. He was a collector of European sculpture, especially images of Hercules, all of which to this day can be seen in this Malibu museum, one of the finest collections ever assembled.

> ## MUCH OF WHAT
> ## I LEARNED CAME FROM
> ## OBSERVATION.

After I moved to North America we kept up our friendship. I never failed to visit him at Sutton Place on my annual visits to the UK. He would show me huge photos (four feet by three feet) that he kept behind his living room couch, of the Malibu project. He begged me to check it out on my return to the States. Because of his fear of flying, having had an extremely bad experience on a commercial aircraft, he never actually got to see this billion-dollar dream Malibu museum enterprise.

Getty taught me to be thrifty. He encouraged me to start an exercise magazine. "Make sure it has service, education and entertainment for the reader." When I observed his lifestyle it made me hungry to one day have a special home of my own. I developed an interest in being a success and having a life of abundance, something my parents had been very much opposed to. Prior to meeting Jean Paul Getty I wouldn't have dared to wish for affluence of any kind.

In 1966 I met Arnold Schwarzenegger. He was 19 and at six-foot-one was around 240 pounds of solid muscle. It was his first time entering the NABBA Universe. Although he didn't win the contest, conceding to Californian Chet Yorton, Arnold was an instant hit because while still only a teenager he was in possession of 20-inch arms!

Even at this young age Arnold had very unusual characteristics.

- He was enormously ambitious.
- He was anxious to learn from everyone.
- He had street smarts and could read people almost instantly.
- He was careful with his money.
- He sought out experts in various fields to absorb information from.
- He had an obvious desire to be rich and famous.
- He was a man of his word when it came to business.

Over the years and right up to the present day, I have been solidly behind Arnold in his ongoing quest for personal achievement, having run a monthly "Arnold Hotline" column in my exercise magazine for 18 years. I have worked

TARGET 20

with Arnold on books and magazines (at one time early on in his career he wrote a regular column for us) for 40 years. Details few people know: Arnold gets more work done in a day than most do in a month, he finds joy and humor in almost everything, and he can get along on only four to five hours' sleep each night. Yes, he always had a strong sexual appetite, a fact that got him in hot water on more than one occasion.

I mentioned that Arnold can read people with enormous accuracy. I do not believe this is a gift we are born with; I believe it is a learned art. Maybe Arnold acquired some of his ability from his Austrian father, who was a police chief in Graz. Police training always involves learning as best as possible how to sum people up. Within minutes Arnold would know what a new acquaintance was all about, what he wanted, whether he was honest, acting a role or just plain innocent.

Arnold always consulted experts in any field he wanted to learn about. No one could listen with more focus. His plan was obvious to those in the bodybuilding world – Arnold would first become the world's undisputed top bodybuilder and then a box office giant in action movies, and follow up as the Governor of California. I wrote some 20 years ago that should it be possible one day that a foreign-born citizen could become president of the United States, Arnold would one day win that role. There are few men

TARGET 20

on this earth who possess Arnold's passion for life; his focus, courage and drive to be the best he can be. For those of you unlucky enough to not know Arnold personally, I promise you he is one in a million. A very unusual man.

Andrew Carnegie, who died in 1919, was a poor immigrant Scottish boy with meager education. He started out as a bobbin boy in a cotton factory and went on to become the world's first billionaire. I never knew Carnegie but that hasn't stopped me from learning from his beliefs and practices. He wrote: "The greatest service you can give to God is to help others." He also believed, and I quote: "The richest heritage a young man can have is to be born into poverty." Being poor had instilled in him the inspiration to overcome all obstacles and achieve almost impossible goals. He believed no degree of impoverishment could hold one back from a successful life. It was after studying Carnegie that Napoleon Hill came up with the line: "Give the public exactly what they want, and you will get what you want."

Another person who was a mentor to me was Ben Weider. Ben was driven by the need for money and the need for recognition. He was an aggressive businessman who worked in synergy with his brother Joe Weider, the founding publisher of *Muscle & Fitness* and *Shape* magazines. What did I learn from Ben? The need to be informed about all aspects of my business. The importance of wearing a stylish jacket and tie for business meetings, and to immediately tackle head on any office problems or situations with individuals or companies that may arise. Ben was not one to walk away from potential trouble. I also learned from both Weider brothers how to publish magazines. In actual fact I learned so well that they ended up imitating some of my own publications. I had a friend, Harry Brooks, who founded the New Day Furniture Company in Manchester, England. He was the first person to offer furniture on the "never-never" (monthly payments, known in the UK as hire-purchase). Harry

> ## THE GREATEST SERVICE YOU CAN GIVE TO GOD IS TO HELP OTHERS.
> *- Andrew Carnegie*

taught me that when offered an attractive item, deal or business opportunity, to: "Say no first and learn to wait." I also came to understand that small monthly payments from a large number of people could add up to one heck of a payday.

When you have a mentor, and yes you can have more than one, you may often get the feeling, "If he can do it, so can I." Accordingly, your enthusiasm can accelerate by leaps and bounds. And when you put your foot to the gas

TARGET 20

pedal, you know what happens. Ralph Waldo Emerson said that nothing great was ever achieved without enthusiasm. It doesn't take much to realize that you should choose something in life that you can be enthusiastic about. A mentor can help in this regard.

Typically a mentor is someone who enjoys sharing his or her ideas. It's nice to be able to sit down with a mentor and chat, but it's not necessary. Andrew Carnegie died at the beginning of the last century, yet his actions and writings can still be admired and learned from. Mentoring can be a switch-around occurrence. I remember answering Arnold Schwarzenegger's ongoing questions when he was in his early 20s. Now things have done a 180. I learn from him. He has been a great businessman, always mixing work with a sense of fun.

Some years ago a 16-year-old boy approached me for a school project. He wanted to interview me on business matters. I agreed and the lengthy interview was recorded. He ended up working for me and ultimately breaking out on his own. Today that same young man, Paul Gardiner, is head of the world's largest food supplement company, doing business in dozens of countries. Today, we get together frequently and learn from each other. Don't let anything stand in the way of finding a successful and caring mentor who enjoys spreading the word and imparting knowledge.

AIM FOR THE BULL

- Your mentor can be anyone in the world.

- Consult experts in their field of expertise.

- Take a personal interest in all aspects of your business.

- Small monthly payments from a large number of people can add up to one heck of a payday.

TARGET 21

You Have to Dream Big and Follow Through With Purpose

"Life consists of what a man is thinking about all day." The words of Ralph Waldo Emerson. True enough, today you are where your thoughts have brought you. Now realize that your future thoughts are where you will be tomorrow.

Good thinkers are always in demand. John C. Maxwell in his best-selling book *How Successful People Think* (Center Street Publishing) quoted Nazi dictator Adolf Hitler as boasting, "What luck for rulers that men do not think."

One of the worst sins to my mind is the common practice of idleness. Men and women who do not want to be bothered to think about anything. You know the kind of person I'm talking about. His mind nibbles at everything and masters nothing. At home in the evening he turns on the TV, gets tired of it, glances through a magazine, flicks the pages, can't get interested and, finally, unable to concentrate on anything, lies back on the couch and falls asleep. At the office he always works on the easiest thing first, and when things are tougher, he puts them aside and starts something else less demanding. He is constantly jumping from one thing to another and each hour becomes routine drudgery, day after day, week after week, and month after month. A brain that rebels at sticking to one thing for more than a few minutes cannot be depended upon to get you anywhere in your years of life.

> NOTHING LIMITS ACHIEVEMENT LIKE SMALL THINKING. NOTHING EXPANDS POSSIBILITIES LIKE UNLEASHED THINKING.

Nothing limits achievement like small thinking. Nothing expands possibilities like unleashed thinking. Unleashing those thoughts and taking the leap to becoming an entrepreneur is exciting and a trifle scary. Fears will invade your mind at every turn. My reason for writing this book is to get you to realize that entrepreneurship is so much more liberating. That's why I want to support you in every way I can. I'm not telling you to quit your job right now. You can still be a proactive achiever while working for a boss. What is somewhat unlikely, however, is that you will become super rich while working for a boss. But success in life cannot just be measured by the size of your bank

TARGET 21

balance. Right now, this minute, this second, this moment I want you to say yes to becoming a possibility thinker. No matter what your vocation, possibility thinking can lead to personal achievement, health, wealth and abundance of all that you cherish. You really can get what you want in life. Those who succeed are thinkers first and proactive second. They talk in terms of I can, I will, and they focus their attention on the job at hand.

> THOSE WHO SUCCEED
> ARE THINKERS FIRST AND
> PROACTIVE SECOND.

Losers are the opposite. They make excuses and throw blame everywhere to justify why things don't work to their advantage. Solid thinkers can realize near-miracles because they believe they can achieve their goals. They push their minds to new levels of forward-thinking optimism. They dream and follow through with purpose. To paraphrase Henry Ford, if you believe you can or believe you can't, you are right!

You cannot hope to rise above the crowd unless you think above the crowd. Sometimes this is best done in groups. Shared thinking can be powerful. When two or more people share a common aim and develop a burning desire for

TARGET 21

attainment, the answer will surely come. Shared thinking is faster than solo thinking. Today shared thinking is easier than ever. We can Google access to thinking partners at the touch of a keyboard. Napoleon Hill referred to this sharing of ideas as employing a Mastermind group, and he used just such a group to help him create his best-selling book, *Think and Grow Rich.*

I often refer to Napoleon Hill as "utterly amazing," and with that statement I am holding back on the praise I really would like to bestow on him. Every published work on personal success and achievement is based in part on the findings of Napoleon Hill. If you haven't read his ground-breaking book, originally published in 1937, I urge you to do so. Also, live Napoleon Hill broadcasts were made way back in the 1940s and these are available through Amazon. The man has been dead for many decades now, yet his words are sheer magic, more important for today's would-be achievers than ever. I urge you to get your hands on this DVD.

Remember it's easy to be a non-thinker. Good creative thinking takes practice, but it can be mastered. It's our way to true north, and our success in living the one life that nature has given us. In the last analysis, success is simply achieving the life you want.

AIM FOR THE BULL

- Think big, above average.

- You cannot hope to rise above the crowd unless you think above the crowd.

- Get hold of some Napoleon Hill recordings.

TARGET 22

Stick With Your Success Plan

Kent Sayre in his excellent book *Unstoppable Confidence!* (McGraw Hill) says, "When I left my corporate job as an engineer in a major semiconductor company, I committed myself mentally, emotionally, and spiritually to living the lifestyle of my dreams by burning all my bridges."

For Kent Sayre there was no chance of going back so he *had* to succeed with his dreams. Anthony Robbins says the same thing: "Success is cutting off all your options for failure." It is very important that you commit 100 percent to achieving your dreams. You can't dilly-dally around with halfhearted attempts. By keeping the door open on a past job, you weaken your determination to give everything to your new vision. Pursuing a single activity and putting everything else on hold is most definitely a solid commitment, and it is one I recommend. You have to be willing to walk away from a secure job or invest your savings into your vision. Taking these risks adds to your determination to succeed. And frequently it is this willingness to go the extra mile that makes the difference between failure and success.

TARGET 22

In similar fashion you should always be willing to stick it out. You chose the road you are on. Stay with it. Frequently when an individual relinquishes his conviction, throws in the towel on a project of his dreams, gives up, surrenders, goes bankrupt, he is "this far" from success. When things seem to be at their worst, give serious thought to holding on. You may be only a millimeter from achieving your goals. Don't quit on the one-yard line; you could be inches from a winning touchdown. Remember that old Richard Nixon line? "When the going gets tough the tough get going." The longer you persist, the more likely your victory. Stick it out!

Some 28 years ago I was running a mail-order business and the company was floundering. I owed considerable money to quite a number of people. The phone was ringing all the time. I couldn't pay my debts. I was encouraged to seek professional help from a law firm specializing in helping companies solve their financial problems. When I met the directors of this company (if I could remember the name I would spell it out right here in bold caps), they told me they would arrange a creditor compromise and that they would see to it the companies I owed money to would agree to being paid .20¢ on the dollar. I was assured that this was common practice, and that the companies would be happy at least to get something rather than nothing if I went bankrupt. I was further instructed to pay myself nothing, and to pay my staff but no one else, not even my

TARGET 22

landlord. And in order to expedite matters I was to hand over power of attorney to this law firm (silly me, eh?). My bank balance went up to $26,000 and the director of this law firm came into my office while I was at lunch, and made himself out a check for exactly $26,000. Yes, he took the lot, leaving me with the same original debts and no cash in the bank. For years I kicked myself over my naiveté, but although most of my friends advised me to declare bankruptcy, I didn't. Instead I got on the phone and talked with the owners of every company to whom I owed money. I explained everything and said that I would pay them a small amount every week until the debts were wiped out. Every one of them agreed and thanked me for contacting them. Within 15 months I had paid everyone off. My lesson was learned. Never give in. If you never quit, you never fail.

I very much like the quote by President Calvin Coolidge, which my mother first brought to my attention when I was in my teens: "Nothing in the world can take the place of persistence. Talent will not; nothing is more common than unsuccessful men with talent. Genius will not; unrewarded genius is almost a proverb. Education will not; the world is full of educated derelicts. Persistence and determination alone are omnipotent."

In my experience high achievers are totally persistent in their journey to success. They simply never give up. It's important to keep striving. That's what life is all about.

> ## LIFELONG HAPPINESS COMES THROUGH STRIVING TO REALIZE YOUR DREAMS.

Lifelong happiness comes through striving to realize your dreams. We are happy when we are growing. That's why those who make millions or win the lottery when they are young should never retire, because when you sit on the beach in the sun you are not achieving. And regular achievement is one of human nature's requirements. Retired people invariably check out on life and die before their time. We all need goals to keep us vibrant and fulfilled.

I like what the world's greatest inventor Thomas Edison said after he invented the electric light bulb: "I had to succeed; I had finally run out of things that didn't work."

TARGET 22

Edison had tried over 6,000 versions before finally coming up with one of the most important inventions ever.

AIM FOR THE BULL

- Force yourself to succeed by committing 100 percent.

- Stay on course through thick and thin.

- Persistence is the most important thing.

- We are happy when we are achieving.

TARGET 23

Reach Your Goals By Speaking Up

They say it's the one thing people fear above all else. What could it be? Skydiving? Caving? Vacationing with the in-laws? No sir, it's public speaking. At least one survey shows that people fear talking in public above death itself. Kind of a severe generalization isn't it? As comedian Jerry Seinfeld joked, this means a person giving a eulogy at a funeral would rather be exchanged for the deceased in the casket. Go figure.

I am well aware that speaking to a group of people can be nerve-racking. As a young teacher I was quite good at it, but then I was only talking in front of a bunch of kids. When I got into business for myself, I became a little more aware of the dynamics of speechmaking. I learned that once you are facing your gathering and ready to speak, you are expected to inform, entertain, educate and totally amuse every person in your audience. To not do so means to fail.

Every person addressing a crowd comes under scrutiny. Whether you are giving a speech in the hopes of winning an election or merely addressing a group of parents at a

TARGET 23

school function, your efforts are dissected from the moment you rise to the second you sit down. Jerry Seinfeld says that because he is famous, when he does his stand-up comedy act most of the audience wants him to fail so they can go home and say, "He bombed."

> # BEING AN AMAZING ORATOR IS NOT ESSENTIAL FOR SUCCESS.

Being an amazing orator is not essential for success. But being reasonably good gives one an edge. Unlike my wife Tosca Reno, who really is an amazing public speaker, giving 30 to 40 seminars a year, I am quite mediocre in the 10 to 12 seminars I give during the same time span. I am never comfortable until I get going and feel the interest of my audience. Initially I dread the thought of addressing a crowd and I find it a challenge to even step on stage. If I get the feeling that the audience is genuinely interested in my words, all ears and truly involved, then you'll find it difficult to get me to leave the stage.

Are you somewhat nervous when you talk in front of others? You should be. A case of nerves keeps your adrenaline flowing. Your thoughts will be clearer – at least they will after you've been talking for a couple of minutes.

TARGET 23

There is a secret to doing a good job. You must know your subject inside and out. You must prepare your speech, write it out, and practice, practice, practice. Say it aloud to your bathroom mirror, in the garden, on the beach looking out to the ocean, down in the basement, in the car, or from a mountaintop. Keep a written copy with you at all times. Pull it out of your pocket at odd moments and read it over and over. Start this process at least three weeks in advance of the day you are to give your speech. Next, put your topic headings on 4x5 cards. Place a few points under each heading. Practice with these because these cards are your

> SAY IT ALOUD
> TO YOUR BATHROOM
> MIRROR, IN THE GARDEN,
> ON THE BEACH LOOKING
> OUT TO THE OCEAN,
> DOWN IN THE BASEMENT,
> IN THE CAR, OR FROM A
> MOUNTAINTOP.

prompters. Once you are up and going, you may well find that you do not need these cards, but the very fact that you have them in your hand while in front of your audience is a confidence builder.

TARGET 23

Should you be using electronic gadgetry, make sure it is all working correctly. Learn how the microphone works and how close it has to be to your mouth to project correctly. Using a screen with PowerPoint? Double-check that it's ready to do its job. It seems to me that half the Power-Point speeches I have attended had initial technical delay problems before the speech could get underway. Have you noticed the same thing?

My mentor, the late genius Napoleon Hill, had this to say about speechmaking, "Know what you are talking about; say it with all the passion and emotion you can muster; and then sit down."

In 2009 I helped 95-year-old fitness guru Jack LaLanne with putting his philosophy of health and fitness into book form. We ended up with *Live Young Forever* (Robert Kennedy Publishing), which proved to be a top seller. Jack helped out by going on numerous talk shows including *Jay Leno, The Doctors* and *Live with Regis and Kelly*. Yes, at 95 the guy was flying all over the country promoting this book. I accompanied Jack to these TV shows and each time he explained that he was nervous before going on TV. But he always put on a stellar performance. He explained that all his life he had been nervous before making a speech or appearance on TV. Now here's a man who produced his own live TV exercise show that ran for 36 years! A man whom I had listened to for nearly 50 years at scores of seminars and appearances. A man who readily admitted that he had a case of the jitters each and every time he had to give a talk in front of an audience. He did also admit that he practiced his talks, and certainly he knew his subject. How about you?

If you make a speech or give a motivational talk to a substantial audience, I suggest you make a recording of it. (Just stick a video camera on a tripod and get someone to press the start button. Make sure the battery is fully charged.) You never know when this footage will become useful. At the very least you will find it interesting to watch as the years roll by.

Always consider what your audience is expecting before you plan your talk. Think of key phrases that might be memorable or amusing. What key points do you want your audience to remember? Should you concentrate on a specific angle or point of view? If you want to hit your target you must know exactly where to aim. You don't want to give too much or too little information. And that information must not be too technical, advanced or over the heads of your audience. Managers, when talking to their employees, often use acronyms and jargon that their audience does not understand. Neither should it be so simple that none of what you say is new to your listeners.

Consider whether you are going to allow questions during your talk ("Put your hand up and I will take your ques-

TARGET 23

tion"), if there will be a question period at the end of your talk or no question period at all. When a question is asked you should repeat it so your audience can hear it clearly. So often, unless a microphone is used, questions from the audience are not heard or understood in their entirety by the rest of the crowd. You should prepare yourself thoroughly if opening up the talk to questions. Give thought to worst-case-scenario questions. Consider the possibility of the hostile question popping up. If you do not understand a question or terminology used by a questioner, then say so. Try, "I'm sorry, could you phrase that question in simpler terms?" or "What do you mean by 'so and so?' I just don't understand the meaning."

> ALWAYS KEEP IN MIND
> THAT YOUR AUDIENCE IS
> THERE BECAUSE OF YOU.

Thinking of using a PowerPoint presentation? Do not merely repeat what's written on your projection image. Your audience doesn't want it repeated verbatim. A better idea is to refer to each point, expanding on it with an original explanation. Just as important as knowing how to make an effective PowerPoint presentation is knowing whether one is appropriate. You may want to give out handouts or worksheets, or nothing at all. Always keep in mind that your audience is there because of you. They want to hear *you* talk and explain your topic. Your visuals (PowerPoint, etc.) are your supplementary aids. You may not need them at all. Some people feel more comfortable using visuals because they help keep them on course, almost like a teleprompter.

If you are truly interested in keeping your audience involved, do not, either in your PowerPoint presentation or your handouts, use excessive text. Limit your words to four to six short lines preceded by a bullet. Know that the secret to public speaking is to have a super-interesting beginning and a strong finish. These are the parts of a speech that are remembered, particularly the beginning because that is when you are being assessed.

> KNOW THAT THE SECRET
> TO PUBLIC SPEAKING
> IS TO HAVE A SUPER
> INTERESTING BEGINNING
> AND A STRONG FINISH.

Beg, borrow or steal a noteworthy beginning. Write it down, practice it until it is word perfect and rolls off the tongue with ease and fluency. Listen to previous speakers; take note of unusual occurrences or recent news items.

TARGET 23

The beginning of your speech is an ideal place to insert something clever and topical. Remember the old line, "A funny thing happened to me on the way to the theater"? It gives the impression that you are totally unrehearsed. As Sheryl Lindsell-Roberts writes in her helpful book *Speaking Your Way to Success* (Houghton Mifflin Harcourt), "Relate a story, ask a thought-provoking question, use a quotation, cite a statistic, show something of interest or tell a joke."

Things can go wrong when making a speech. The microphone can fail, as can the PowerPoint equipment. The audience can be very sparse. (Ever spoken to just three people when you were expecting 300?) You could face an audience set on disagreeing with your opinions using loud comments. Hey, it happens.

Unlikely as these things are, it is best to prepare as well as possible. Visit the area where you will be making your talk. Try and work out where you will stand. Will there be a lectern? I recently attended a function where four women spoke onstage. There was a dreadful overhead light above the lectern, making the speakers look positively evil. One woman had obviously done her homework. When she came onstage she positioned herself near a flattering light that she had taken the trouble to discover before the speechmaking began.

TARGET 23

On the night of your event, visit the toilet before going to the speech-making site. If you feel the adrenaline pounding, run in place, lifting your knees high for 30 seconds. Speak loudly for 30 seconds to loosen and lubricate your vocals. Glance at your notes, going over the salient points, take a few deep breaths and stride out to your audience … facing them and allowing your personality the freedom to shine. Knock 'em dead!

AIM FOR THE BULL

- Preparation is the key to good public speaking.

- Make a video recording of every speech.

- Make sure stage lighting, sound and PowerPoint equipment is in working order.

TARGET 24

Utilize Other People's Brains

To utilize other people to help you achieve your goals is an enormously important concept. Napoleon Hill called it the "Mastermind" approach, and he defined it as: "Coordination of knowledge and effort, in a spirit of harmony, between two or more people, for the attainment of a definite purpose."

Today, of course, all serious businesses have a boardroom where regular meetings are held. Naturally, the people you have in your Mastermind group have to be selected with care. Basically, you want trusted individuals who have more knowledge and experience than you have on the aspects of your aspirations and ideals. Your group of individuals must have enthusiasm because enthusiasm keeps the wheels of creativity turning. It's team playing. Your role is always to head the boardroom table to set the agenda, control the meeting by keeping it on track and to encourage, but moderate, free thinking. And of course it doesn't have to be a boardroom. It can be your kitchen table. If two or more people are in attendance then we can call it a Mastermind meeting. Yes, you and a friend talking ideas can come up with a monumental amount of useful and in-

TARGET 24

novative concepts. Once a Mastermind alliance is formed the group must remain active and meet with definite goals towards achieving a common objective.

I spent a good 20 years in business without a boardroom, and growth was relatively slow. When I started utilizing other people's brains, knowledge and ingenuity, my business doubled, and then tripled. Today I have three boardrooms, and men and women with enough knowledge and enthusiasm to fill all three.

Always remember: When several people with a burning desire to achieve anything get together, then they will move mountains. It's true. A group of minds working in unison, functioning in harmony, can, through that alliance, create a forum that can bring magical and brilliant ideas to the fore. Ideas that can help you achieve your definite purpose in life.

One way to utilize other people's knowledge and expertise is through books. Myself, I have scores of books on personal achievement. I love reading about how others have achieved their individual successes. Biographies, especially autobiographies, are a great way to learn. Just think, a man or woman can spend a whole lifetime struggling to achieve and write about all the trials and tribulations of their entrepreneurial adventures and you can read and learn all about those 50-odd years of activity in one book. In two or three

TARGET 24

days you can learn about all the hazards, uncertainties and joys of their careers. Books are wonderful.

> IN TWO OR THREE DAYS
> YOU CAN LEARN ABOUT
> ALL THE HAZARDS,
> UNCERTAINTIES
> AND JOYS OF THEIR
> CAREERS. BOOKS ARE
> WONDERFUL.

Currently my painting career, which I practice under my late father's name, Wolfgang Kals (wolfgangkals.com), is taking off, and much of it is due to the fact that I have been reading books on my favorite artists: Picasso, Basquiat, Johns, Hockney, Matisse, Bacon, Moore, Van Gogh, Cezanne, etc. for years. And I've learned from everyone. This habit has translated into me having more knowledge of art and artists and has directly improved my art to the extent that collectors are showing more interest every month. My paintings are not cheap, but last month alone I sold three and one other canvas was put on hold. It's been exciting. But then my best friend took the wind out of my sails by saying that collectors are only interested in my work because at 73 years of age I could "kick the bucket" any day, and the paintings would multiply in value overnight. Hey! I'm not ready to go below ground just yet, thank you.

TARGET 24

> ## BUSINESS PROBLEMS ARE THE COMMON THREAD OF MOST MASTERMIND MEETINGS.

But back to books. They are utterly invaluable to your progress. And fortunately there are a ton of books on every subject imaginable. I have heard it said that one has to learn from firsthand experience, and that reading about something or hearing it from a friend is useless. There is a grain of truth in this, but believe me you can learn from books. I have learned, and I know many (no exaggeration) people who have changed their lives around after reading books and magazines. It's all a matter of attitude. You can learn how to exercise from books, you can learn about the world's religions. You can learn how to cook, sew, paint, how to relate to others, how to speak in public, how to revise your life, shed excess fat, moonwalk, build a house, sail a boat. A million things, invaluable, priceless treasures can be learned from the printed page. A single paragraph read, understood, assimilated and acted upon can change your life. Never doubt it!

Masterminding does not have to take place in the boardroom. It can be just as valuable on the golf course, or at the club, even the gym between bench presses and lateral raises. The car, too, is an amazing place to share views and brainstorm. You have a captive audience. And you can even learn from others when there's no one else in the car. Stick in a personal achievement CD. There are literally hundreds available from my favorite company Nightingale/Conant (nightingale.com/ 1-800-525-9000). I strongly recommend you check out their site. Whether you actually invest in any of their CDs is up to you, but you certainly will, in my opinion, get your money's worth if you do.

A group of individuals trying to solve problems, be innovative and allow their creative juices to flow can bring a focus and depth of discovery that one person alone cannot easily duplicate. The basic philosophy of group meetings is that more can be achieved in less time when people work together in an atmosphere of trust, rationality, passion and derring-do. Little wonder that every company of significance holds regular meetings among the staff, oftentimes bringing in a guest speaker to offer a fresh perspective.

Don't have a boardroom? Arrange phone conferences to iron out ideas, broadcast views, give feedback, share resources and generally discuss how to better facilitate your pathway to achieving personal goals and fulfilling your dreams. A Mastermind group can be enormously powerful, and it can be held with people of your own industry or profession or with people from the non-business community. Business problems are the common thread of most

TARGET 24

Mastermind meetings. However, personal issues can also be shared in a group environment. My friend, fitness guru Jack LaLanne, had a habit very early on in his life of seeking out experts on any subject on which he needed to know more. He would ask questions – lots of questions.

In forming your mastermind group, it is a good idea to select men and women who know considerably more than you do on the topic under discussion. I feel an ideal group should consist of five people, last one-and-a-half hours and be held in an area as private and free of distractions as possible. Each participant should have pen and paper or a small computer to record interesting suggestions. Full attention has to be given to each point of view, and all points of view should be shared even though the speaker may feel his or her idea is a little weird or loopy. There has to be a relationship among all in your group. Strangers cannot easily or quickly relate. When there is a common thread of friendship in your group, conversation will flow effortlessly. Magical ideas will materialize.

AIM FOR THE BULL

- Enthusiastic groups of people can be hugely creative.

- Don't underestimate the importance of books and magazines.

- All points of view should be shared.

- When I started utilizing other people's brains, knowledge and ingenuity, my business doubled and then tripled.

TARGET 25

You Never Know When Life is Going to Hit You Below the Belt

Tough times come to us all, not just in love or business but in life itself. We can't get away from this. Both my parents got through life with a combination of hard work and tranquility. As schoolteachers they were always employed in a profession. I admired them for their integrity and normalcy even though I couldn't follow in their footsteps. I had an appetite for more. But they were happy, honest and content.

I wasn't as lucky when it came to a life of serenity. One fall day in 1998, I was cheering on my 10-year-old son Braden in his last soccer match of the season. His team won 6-4. I took the whole team out to Pizza Hut for a celebratory meal, and after the loads of happy cheers and laughter we said our goodbyes and went on our way. I took one of Braden's friends home and then, driving back to our house on a country road it happened. A black pickup truck, overtaking a car, came speeding down a hill toward me on my side of the road. I had only one choice – to turn my convertible off the road and into the ditch. The car turned over

TARGET 25

and trapped Braden underneath. I was knocked out cold. Neighbors came out of surrounding houses and stared, and although Braden's arm was sticking outside of the overturned sports car, no one thought to lift the car off him (something that could easily be done since there were more than a dozen people standing around). Consequently, Braden's breathing was terminated by the weight of the car and oxygen was prevented from getting to his brain. He experienced an oxygen-deprived head injury. My wife, Lynda, and I spent over a year at Sick Kids Hospital in Toronto, hoping every day that he would get better. Then one day, 13 months after the accident, he had a third brain scan. From a distance of some 30 yards or more, Lynda heard two nurses commiserating over the results of the scan. She concluded that his injury was global and that there was no chance of any recovery. When my wife heard this she went out, bought herself a bottle of wine and threw herself under a subway train. The note she left in her handbag said that she had given up her life in the hope that she could help Braden from the "other side." The final line, directed to our daughter, read: "Chelsea, I love you and I will always love you."

I was left with a five-year-old daughter to bring up and care for. Today as I write this, Chelsea, at 18 years of age, is a fine young woman currently enjoying life, doing well at university and popular among her friends.

> ## FACTS DO NOT CEASE TO EXIST BECAUSE THEY ARE IGNORED.
> *- Aldous Huxley*

A further year was spent with Braden at a rehab center and then he came home with 24-hour nursing care. He was unable to move. He couldn't talk and was fed through a G-tube in his stomach. He spent his time lying on a comfortable bed and was put in his wheelchair every few hours for some variety to his day. Needless to say these events with my brave boy were devastating. Braden died of pneumonia, in the middle of my writing this book, at the age of 23.

And the truck that caused the accident sped off before police and ambulances arrived, never to be located.

TARGET 25

Most of the motivational tapes I've listened to and books I have read espouse the theory that one should face adversity, that when bad things happen there is always a balance that takes place. Even when losing a loved one there is a seed of compensation that nature provides. It doesn't come immediately but it does come.

I agree up to a point, but the events that took place as a result of my car accident can never be *balanced* by any event. It is simply a huge tragedy, the haunting recurrent thoughts of which still dominate my everyday thinking. I will miss my beautiful son until my dying day.

Stress is something we all endure. Some of us deal with it effectively while others allow it to interfere with their work, their dreams and aspirations. At times when the going gets tough stress becomes part of the equation. But being stressed doesn't help anything to advance except the size of your ulcers or the rise in your blood pressure. Stressed-out people fail to see solutions or make sensible decisions and can barely think clearly. Their relationships with coworkers or family members can become strained to the breaking point. I know all this so very well.

You have to do everything in your power to keep the evils of stress out of your life. And don't allow your anxiety to spread among others. Nothing good will come of it. You have to take full possession of your mind. You become what you think about. As Aldous Huxley told us, "Facts do not cease to exist because they are ignored."

If a relationship is seriously coming to an end, consider walking away rather than getting down and dirty and fighting it out. This is important for the two of you. So many couples have gone from adoring each other to holding repeated "spitting nails" arguments that can only do harm to both parties. If it's dead, walk away.

Fighting a downturn in your business or service can seem difficult. It can be uncomfortable to admonish an employee. You may be reticent about asking your bank for a line of credit. The telling of your staff that there will be a temporary 10 percent cut in their pay until things turn around can seem daunting. However, a downturn in the economy or a change in the way things are done in your business can necessitate change, and prompt change at that.

You can't let rejection ruin your day. I know it can be pretty upsetting when you ask a special person for a date and you get a flat, "No thank you. I like you but I'm dating someone right now." Or the somewhat worse, "Sorry, but I do my laundry on Saturday nights." But believe me we all get rejected from time to time. I can well remember as a teenager not being picked for a football team, and when I was in amateur theater I recall not getting a lead part in a play that I desperately hoped for. But so what if you don't get that pay raise at work or your new product idea is soundly rejected? Who cares? Tomorrow is another day, the first day of the rest of your life. A time of promise and adventure. Also bear in mind that the old adage, "When one door closes another opens," carries a degree of truth.

When times are tough you have to be willing to pay the price. It may be that you have to work an extra hour each day or that you have to create a support group where you meet once a week to brainstorm new ways of beating the downturn. Will you need to advertise more, or more creatively? What about delegating your less urgent "busy work" to others while you concentrate on the real job of greater importance?

> ## WHEN THE GOING GETS TOUGH, THE TOUGH GET GOING.
> *– Richard Nixon*

Consider that tough times may have come your way because you've been doing something wrong, making a mistake, getting into trouble. You've been digging yourself into a hole. The answer is to take stock of yourself and make some changes. Don't increase the intensity of what you have been doing wrong. If you have dug yourself into a hole you need a ladder, not a shovel with which to continue digging deeper and deeper.

TARGET 25

When a problem comes your way consider whether it is something that should be addressed right away or left alone for a while. While hiding from a problem never does any good, sometimes focusing on it can make it seem more important than it really is.

You never know when life is going to hit you below the belt. One day you're sailing on smooth ocean waters, cutting through the sea with a full sail, and the next a storm appears from nowhere, tossing you about, tearing sails, battering waves threatening to take you to the bottom of the ocean, and you feel the worst of life, that unsavory feeling that all is lost. The only answer is to carry on as best as possible. Scour the very depths of your mind to figure out the best solution and then follow through with appropriate action. As Richard Nixon said, when the going gets tough, the tough get going. Never give up. And lo and behold a new day; better times are around the corner.

AIM FOR THE BULL

- Be serious about controlling stress.

- Don't allow rejection to cause pain.

- A seed of something good comes from every disaster.

TARGET 26

Take Action.
Avoid These 7 Fears

We all have fears. Some worse than others. Basic fears like that of the dark, of high places, of drowning or falling are no-brainers, but there are plenty of other fears less obviously defined. For example, feelings like jealousy, hate and the urge for revenge may be rooted in the emotion of fear.

You can conquer abnormally atypical fears by facing them head on, considering the ludicrous beliefs that have led to your particular set of fears. When I was in school, in my early years of mastering swimming and diving, I accepted a dare from a fellow classmate and dived off the top board at the local swimming pool. Not knowing what I was doing, I failed to close my eyes or tuck my head between my shoulders as I entered the water. Smack! My wide-open eyes received the full force of the pool's surface. I was temporarily blinded for several minutes. That was enough to set up an extended fear of diving that stayed with me for years. Today I've faced that fear by diving off the side of a pool. There will be no climbing to the top board, that's for sure. While I may not have beaten the fear entirely, I lessened the apprehension considerably, and so can you.

Don't Become a Hypochondriac

According to the Mayo Clinic's deductions, the belief of illness is not a true delusion – that is, the person can accept the possibility that he or she may not in fact have a serious disease. Hypochondria is instead the abnormal fear of illness, causing an obsessive preoccupation.

We should all be concerned about our health and try to prevent illness by exercising regularly, eating clean and getting adequate sleep and rest, but to allow unreasonable apprehension to creep into your psyche will not benefit you in any way.

> I STILL GO TO THE
> OFFICE FIVE DAYS A
> WEEK TO MAKE BOOKS
> AND MAGAZINES.
> I LIVE LIFE WITH
> MORE PASSION THAN
> EVER. HOW ABOUT YOU?

Don't Allow Fear of Competition to Stall Your Plans for Success

Competition is everywhere. Don't fear it; embrace it. Even if you came up with an amazing new moneymaking invention, chances are it would be copied before you knew it! Think you can get around the problem by patenting your invention? No way. A slightly different product will get around the problem. Competition invariably serves to build a bigger pie. Think about all the cookbooks out there… diet books, exercise books and so on. The pie is enormous, all built by competition. Every worthwhile product benefits in the midst of a competitive environment.

Don't Let Revenge be a Part of Your Life's Mission

When someone wrongs me, I simply refuse to be associated with them anymore. I do not seek revenge. When someone steals while working for me, either at home or at the office, I simply terminate them without a second's hesitation. I do not seek revenge. Whether they steal a postage stamp or a computer, they are instant history.

I wasn't always so forgiving. In my 20s I had a dry cleaning service totally ruin my one and only, very much prized, teal-colored leather jacket. To make matters worse they claimed there was nothing wrong with it. When I pointed to a photograph showing how the original looked, they denied it was the same jacket. When I tried to put it on, I couldn't even get my arms into the sleeves. I thought about little else for weeks, phoning several times a day, demanding my costs for a new jacket be met. All to no avail. In the end I arranged to see the owner face to face at his dry cleaning store. He gave me all of 20 seconds and swore I wouldn't get a penny of compensation, concluding his conversation with "F-you!" I was so incensed that with a sweep of my arm I brushed his cash register from the counter to the ground and walked out of his store.

Yes, taking revenge has its rewards but later that night I had a visit from the police. After much banter it was agreed that I would not pay for the cash register damage, and he wouldn't pay for the ruined leather jacket. I went through weeks of stomach-turning hassle and trauma for nothing. Forget revenge and live your life that much freer of angst.

Don't Fear the Aging Process

Why people think that when they reach the ripe old age of 40 they are going to dry up and blow away I don't know. Research has shown that the most results-producing years are frequently during the ages of 65 to 80.

There are many advantages that come our way as we age, not least of which is the accumulation of experience that we have over our younger friends, business associates and acquaintances. We have been there, done that!

With the added years comes wisdom. Invariably we have concluded that worry by itself solves nothing. We have learned to be unhurried and to tackle problems that others may deem insurmountable with calm and common sense.

TARGET 26

Whether you are coming up to 40 or 80, no problem. As I approach my mid 70s, I enjoy virtually every minute I have on God's Earth. I love my family and my life more every day. I balance my exercise time in the gym with my oil painting and writing, and I still go to the office five days a week to make books and magazines. I live my life with more passion than ever. How about you?

> FORGET REVENGE
> AND LIVE YOUR LIFE
> THAT MUCH FREER
> OF ANGST.

Don't Allow the Words of Naysayers to Affect Your Judgments
In 1937 my hero Napoleon Hill was commissioned by billionaire steel magnate Andrew Carnegie to spend a full 20 years writing a book on building a success philosophy for life, without any financial compensation. (Carnegie gave Mr. Hill contact names of several presidents and literally hundreds of successful business entrepreneurs, but no payment.) Napoleon's friends and family openly scorned him for accepting the assignment. Fortunately Mr. Hill's resolve to complete the job was strong enough that he paid no attention to the naysayers. *Think and Grow Rich* is the

forerunner of every how-to book on living your best life ever published and has sold almost four million copies in North America alone.

There is nothing wrong with listening to advice from others... once. But do not listen to repeated disparaging discourse. Dissect carefully what others have to say, and then make up your own mind according to your own beliefs, experiences and convictions. In all probability you have given 10 times the thought they have to any subject or project under consideration, and therefore the final decision is rightfully yours and yours alone.

> ## IF YOU HAVE INTEGRITY YOU HAVE NOTHING TO FEAR, BECAUSE YOU HAVE NOTHING TO HIDE.

Don't Permit Hate to Guide Your Actions

One of my competitors in the magazine business, Joe Weider, told me once that hate was a great motivator. He has a point. If you use hate to stir up your old resolve, to work harder, to think sharper, then his argument is valid. But do we really want to stoop to this level of having to look for all-consuming hate in order to advance ourselves as life's successes unfold?

TARGET 26

Have you caught yourself secretly hoping that someone you know would fail? Maybe that someone was a sibling, a neighbor, colleague or best friend? It happens. Certainly you are not wishing they get killed on the road, die in a house fire or encounter other serious bad luck, but your inner hopes are that they don't become more successful than you. This type of thinking is something we have to fight against. I urge you to think in the opposite way. Wish every one of your friends the utmost success. There is room for us all. Their success will add to your own achievements, I promise.

Don't Allow Fear of the Rules to Wreck Your Life

That tiny voice inside of us, our conscience, is always reminding us of what's right and wrong. The daily news is there to remind us. Individuals are getting into trouble over and over again because they made bad decisions.

In the beginning of my serious business activity, around 1970, I neglected to file tax papers. I was so keen to build my enterprise that I let one year slip into another without filing. Naturally this soon caught up with me and I was assessed at owing a bunch of back tax. A lien was put on my house and ultimately when I sold the house, half the money had to go to the taxman. When I was finally up to date, I had an amazing feeling of relief. My advice is to always pay your taxes and follow the rules of proper business etiquette, and you will always have peace of mind. If

TARGET 26

you have integrity you have nothing to fear, because you have nothing to hide.

As you pass through the years of your life there will be all kinds of opportunity to take advantage of people, family, friends and colleagues, and in a variety of situations. Don't do anything that your conscience tells you is wrong.

One time, at the conclusion of a children's soccer game, I found a fat wallet lying on the ground. Nobody saw me pick it up. I could have kept it and the contents and no one would be any the wiser. As I counted over $400 I recalled some words of my mother: "Just because you are certain you can get away with something you know is wrong, it is no reason to be dishonest." Without a second thought I tracked down the owner via a plumber's bill in the wallet, drove to his home and made his day much brighter. When you do the right thing over and over again every day, your day too can be brighter.

TARGET 26

AIM FOR THE BULL

- Face fears head on.

- Welcome competition; it builds a bigger pie.

- Keep negative people out of your life.

- Remember: You get wiser as you age.

TARGET 27

Get on With Life. It's Zooming Past

What have you been doing in life up to now? Have you been enjoying yourself? Or has life been a bit of a letdown? Whatever the case I'm sure you've had your share of disappointments, mistakes, sad events, accidents … but there have been happy times too, right? Great times, in fact. Fun and successful times, I'm sure.

Looking ahead, do you want more out of life? It's only natural if you do. Consider what you have learned from this book. This minute, I want you to renew your interest in this book's advice and make a bond with me. I want some action from you – now, right away. Whether it's Googling a name, phoning a friend, checking on an asking price for an office space or potential store, interviewing an expert, looking for information on a particular product or checking out franchise opportunities. I want you to commit now. It is possibly the most important decision you'll ever make. Certainly it will change your destiny. Your life from this moment on can take on a new meaning; glorious, incredible success and the sheer joy that goes with it.

I need some sort of action that gets you started on a new paradigm of super-successful conduct. Realize that at last you are waking up from a deep sleep and becoming tuned in to the truth about how to begin on the journey from where you are today to where you want to be in the future. Although it's great to have enough money to do the things you want to do, it's not all about money. Money can't make you thinner, healthier, fitter, more popular or loved. It isn't the cure you're looking for. So what is the answer? It is to live passionately with enthusiasm. To find a purpose in life that is totally rewarding. A job that just cannot be described as work. To love and be loved. To excel at what you do and be appreciated. And yes, when you help people find what they want, you will get what you want – an abundance of financial capital is part of that equation. We have itemized what wealth cannot do, but money does allow for bigger and better things. It allows you to help others, to share the wealth. It makes travel to anywhere an option, a treat that most people can only dream of.

> YOU CAN DO WHATEVER
> YOU WANT, BE
> WHATEVER YOU WANT.

TARGET 27

By following my advice I believe you have an enormous chance of completely changing your life for the better. You can do whatever you want, be whatever you want. An extraordinary life lies ahead for you. Keep your thoughts positive. Keep your values intact. Your destiny is in your hands.

Your health is super important to your quality of life. I could write for days on eating for maximum health. My wife Tosca Reno is an expert on healthy eating – knowing which foods strip you of excess fat and offer you the best possible health – and delivers what you need to know to live a lifestyle of eating clean. Go to her sites toscareno.com and eatcleandiet.com for information about her.

> TALL OR SHORT, FAT OR THIN, YOUNG OR NOT SO YOUNG, YOUR LIFE CAN BE ANYTHING YOU WANT IT TO BE.

You cannot be healthy and expect a trouble-free existence by following the average North American diet. Eat organic, live, vital foods that are created through the natural interaction of the sun, soil, air and water. Fill your plate with lean meats, fish, fruits, vegetables and whole grains. Start every meal with a salad and take fruit for dessert. Chocolate-covered doughnuts should not be part of your diet!

Sleep and rest are vital to your health. You need a minimum of seven hours' sleep. Most need eight hours. You need to consciously relax at different times during the day, especially after meals. If you find yourself running around all day, sighing at everything you have to do, then you are driving yourself into illness.

There are a ton of books on the importance of exercise. Without going into details here (this is not a book on body sculpting) let it be understood that exercise should be tailored to an individual's fitness level and this can be attained only by working with a professional who is well versed in the practical side of physical training.

Live every day as though it were your last. Life will take on new meaning. Learn to enjoy every second. Laugh, play, work and give thanks for all you have. Laughing and living with joy are medicine for the soul. Get to bed on time and get up early. Remember what your granny said all those years ago, "Early to bed and early to rise makes a man [or woman] healthy, wealthy and wise."

We're at the end of these chapters now. Quick, promise yourself your dreams are not going to vanish the second you close this book and put it back on the shelf. Remem-

ber my ironclad conviction that you, yes *you,* can do anything, and make sure you hold that same conviction, because it's true.

Tall or short, fat or thin, young or not so young, your life
can be just as you want it to be. Your destiny is in your
hands. Don't fritter it away as the days, weeks and months
pass by. We here in the real world will never get a second
chance to live life to the fullest.

Adopt the principles I've laid out. Don't let your current
level of enthusiasm fade. You really, really can do it. I'm
with you all the way. I envy your chances.

AIM FOR THE BULL

- Take some action now.

- Money is not an automatic means to happiness.

- This book really is your key to success.

- I envy your chances.

INTERVIEWS

The following five interviews of self-made millionaires were made personally by myself to give *Bull's Eye* readers an idea of how "ordinary" individuals started their own businesses from scratch ... ultimately taking each to multi-million-dollar status.

Bob Proctor

Bob Proctor is one of the world's most celebrated teachers of personal development. Bob was a primary contributor to *The Secret*, available in book and DVD format, by Rhonda Byrne.

Bob is a humble man. A high-school dropout, he earned a living as a cleaner before rising to his true potential. He describes himself today as a teacher of universal laws. Bob instructs that there is more to wealth than just money, but he is not just a spiritual teacher. He believes that wealth is attainable by everyone, and that everyone who wants to should be financially rich! Bob firmly believes that your finances, relationships, health and spiritual growth can explode with possibilities if you adopt the correct approach.

RK: Richard Branson says he's having fun and Donald Trump says he loves making deals. Do you go after money, or are you focused on the passion for helping people, letting the financial stuff take care of itself?

BP: I do what I do because I love doing it. I used the information I teach to change my own life. I became so fascinated with it that I wanted to share it. I would've given it away for nothing, except that didn't work so I started to sell it. I think money is a symptom of doing things the right way. It's a reward for service rendered. I'll sometimes set a money objective for a project, and then I move back and focus on that. It's really got to be worthwhile and offer value. I think one of the tricks is to find out what people really want, and most people don't really know what they want. Most people are settling for what they think they can get. They don't realize they can have what they want. My objective is to help people think about what they really want, and help them achieve their goals.

How did you get involved with helping people enjoy a more successful life? How did it first start?

It started with me when I was on the fire department in East York in Canada. That was the best job I'd ever had. I had no formal education, no business experience and I was in debt. A fellow I met told me I should buy *Think and Grow Rich* by Napoleon Hill and study it, and follow what he suggested. That changed things for me. It got me thinking I could really do something where before I was thinking I couldn't. I've never stopped reading it.

INTERVIEWS

Think and Grow Rich, what a great book.

I read it and started to do what it said. And my results changed so dramatically. I started to do anything honest to earn money. Someone said there was good money cleaning floors, so I said, "I'm not proud, I'll clean floors." In less than five years I was cleaning offices in Toronto, Montreal, Cleveland, Boston, Atlanta and London, England. It took me a while to realize I wasn't in the cleaning business at all. So I eventually left the cleaning biz and started with personal development.

What came first – your books or your speaking engagements?

Oh, the book, the programs. I'm actually, in my genetic nature, very quiet and shy. But I knew so much about this, I had to know why I changed. Most people don't know why they change, why they do well. It took me nine years. I just kept studying and I finally put the pieces of the puzzle together. I had a very strong desire to teach it, but I was afraid to get up in front of an audience. I once saw Bill Gove speak in Chicago in the '60s. He was considered the Frank Sinatra of speakers. And so I made up my mind to get him to teach me to do what he was doing.

Did you always know you'd be successful?

No, I was actually shocked by what was happening to me as I was reading *Think and Grow Rich*. But I was doing what was in the book, and I think because of that I've always focused more on what I'm doing than what I'm getting. But when you give people what they want, you get what you want.

What was the turning point?
When I refocused on doing the best job I could do. Up until then I was doing whatever I could to get by.

That's so true. You just give people everything you can and be the best you can, and it comes back to you. Emerson said that's the law of cause and effect. What you put out, you get back. The truth is the second you put it out you get it back. It's energy that's flowing from your brain. We give it direction and our brain takes on an equal amount of like energy as we put it out. We don't have to worry about staying positive; we just have to worry about doing good. We're surrounded by energy. It's flowing through us; you can actually photograph the energy leaving a person. We get to choose what we do with it. J. Martin Kohe wrote a little book called *Your Greatest Power*. It's just a little tiny book. It promotes that the greatest power is the power to choose.

Did you have any failures?
I've had all kinds of failures. I'm still having them. I think that's a part of winning. In the little book by Price Pritchett, *You²*, he says a rocket fails on its way to the moon. It's off course more than it's on course. That happens to us. We make mistakes… then correct, correct, correct; we're for-

ever correcting. I believe there's perfection within us. It's a matter of bringing that perfection to the surface. And if you think you're not going to make mistakes, you're wrong. You'll hear a parent saying to a little child that's letting go of the table and is going to walk: "Be careful or you might fall." The kid is going to fall. He's going to whack his head, he's going to cry, you're going to cry, but he's going to get up and keep on going. Falling is a natural part of walking and temporary failure is part of winning.

That's a self correction and it's like a baby reaching for something but failing to grasp it. But with repeated correction they eventually succeed.

There's a great book out, I just started to read it: *Talent is Overrated* by Geoff Colvin – it's a great book. He talks about deliberate practice. You've got to really put a lot of effort into it. He says it comes easy to some people, but he hasn't found it came easy to anyone who really made it. You have to love what you're doing and work hard at it.

That's interesting. People who are called geniuses, often it's because they started practicing the skill at four years of age and put time in it – 1,000 or 10,000 hours, or whatever.

Practice makes perfect.

Napoleon Hill, author of *Think and Grow Rich*, said when you pray with real intensity that your prayers

INTERVIEWS

will be answered.

I believe that but not in the sense that he wrote it. I believe the mind is working with energy all the time and you can build an idea in your consciousness, and if you get emotionally involved with that idea you stay in that vibration – the idea dictates that vibration and the vibration dictates what you attract.

Isn't prayer like convincing yourself subconsciously?
If you believe it, it's the intent of the idea. You're dealing with laws. The universe is an orderly universe. That's what I actually teach. I once heard somebody say that praying is what most people do between prayers, and I think he's right.

Can you name three people who've helped you, or from whom you have studied or learned?
I've had seven. Ray Stanford, Leland Val Van De Wall, Earl Nightingale, Lloyd Conant, Bill Gove, Dr. C. Harry Roder and Thomas Troward – he's been dead for years.

Is one more important than the others?
No. At the time they were helping me they were all vitally important.

The books that you've read – have you kept them?
Almost all of them.

Do you revisit any of your books?
Well, you change when you read. When you read a good

book through a second time, you don't see something that you didn't see before; you see something in yourself that wasn't there before. We gain awareness. As we become more aware, we see more.

I agree, reading books through twice or even seeing a movie twice is sometimes more exciting. You absorb things you hadn't before. Can anyone be successful?
I believe they can. I used to go into Kingston Penitentiary and teach the inmates what I was studying. I went in there one Saturday a month for five years, almost every month. There's one guy I'm thinking of. His name was Joe Gardner; he had shot a man in a holdup. He was a bad guy. He had been in solitary confinement for seven years when I met him. After our time together, he got out on a special ticket, and he had to report to the city police every week and to the Mounties every month. He and his wife got back together. She'd had a baby while he was in prison, and he treated that little girl like she was his own. I opened an office in England, and I went to the authorities and asked them to give him back his passport. He came with me to London and I had him running my office over there. He never got in trouble again. He had totally reshaped his life. Yes, I believe anyone can be successful, but they really have to want it. I think Joe Gardner changed because he could see that I believed in him. I could see beyond what he could see in himself. A good coach or mentor will do that for you.

INTERVIEWS

Did you ever give up?
No, but I did quit in 1980 for about nine months. I was running seminars all over North America, lugging my stuff all over the place, doing everything myself. I was really tired. I was conducting a seminar for Metropolitan Life at the Sheraton in Los Angeles. After the talk these two guys came up to me. "Man, we've never seen anything like it. You had the audience captivated. They never moved; never shuffled their feet or went to the bathroom for over three hours," they said. I met up with these guys again in Portland and they told me: "You shouldn't be lugging your own stuff from state to state. You should have a limo pick you up at the airport wherever you go."

At the time I didn't know much about business and to make a long story short I ended up working under contract, with them owning the company. It was a bad deal. I left the seminar business for nine months and did nothing.

Finally a company in Ottawa called me and asked me to speak at a convention. At first I refused, but after giving it some thought I agreed. I was back in business.

What was the key factor that made you successful without which you would not have made it? Was there something that came along?
I know exactly what it was. I started to believe in me. Until you start believing in yourself, I don't think you're ever going to have real success. I think that's a prerequisite to success.

INTERVIEWS

I got my wife Tosca believing in herself – she's sold over two million books now.

If you don't believe in yourself, you're not going to do the things you need to in order to become a success.

Most people I know, even those with a lot of money, complain they don't have enough money. They can't pay their bills or they're barely able to survive. Whether they're getting $300 per week or $5,000 a week they say, "I want more money, I want more money."

Well I think really successful people always want more money. Money is the medium of exchange for other people's products and services. I think you've got to be building and growing. If you're not growing, you're dying. It's create or disintegrate, so you're either going in one direction or another. And money is an absolute essential to growth. I'm always doing things that cost more money than I've got, so I have to earn more to do more, and I'm just interested in expanding. I'm not interested in going the other way.

My parents poo-pooed money. They were schoolteachers, and they said, "Why would you want to do this Robert?" (with magazines or anything I undertook) "Teaching is a good profession. Stay with it – we've made a good living." And they had a small, comfortable home and were happy. I realized I did want more.

You see, I've studied that. And it has a religious connotation to it that goes way back, where the religious rogues were saying, "Money is no good – give it to us and we'll give it to God." Most people grow up with the idea that money is not good. The truth is money is very good because it will extend the service you can render far beyond your own physical needs. You can be generous to others, but you can also be more creative. Try being creative without money, and your creativity is going to be stunted.

Zig Ziglar said it right; he said, paraphrasing, Money is not that important, but it's kind of up there with oxygen. I think money is important. A lot of people run it down who don't have it.
Yes, people who haven't got money are the ones who say it's not important. People who have money know what it is and understand how it's used.

What are the impediments that hold people back from being successful?
Well, there's only one and it's ignorance. Ignorance is the only problem in the world. It causes wars; it causes all the problems we've got. Now if you go beyond that, it's paradigms, it's the conditioning in our subconscious mind that keeps us stuck where we are. Most people don't understand paradigms; they don't understand how they're formed or how they can be changed, so their lives never really change and it stays much the same, all the way through.

INTERVIEWS

When you give your seminars, people get all excited: "I'm going to do this now, I'm going to do it." Do you have a feeling in your head that a good proportion of those people won't actually make that step and follow through with it? They get excited at that moment and then it goes away?

I frequently tell them that out of 100, probably only two or three are going to go out and act on it. However, what I teach doesn't just get people excited. It's not motivation – it's really education in the true sense of the word. I help them understand the relationship of the mind to the body. I help them understand how to alter what's going on in their minds, how their minds function.

In your case, how is most of your income made?

Speaking engagements, seminars, coaching programs. We train people as consultants with our material.

Do you have an Internet site?

We have a number of them: bobproctor.com; insightoftheday.com; sixminutestosuccess.com; lscorporate.com; bobproctorcoaching.com

What about a newsletter – do you have a newsletter?

In a sense, we do. We send out a positive quote each day and on Friday we put a story with it. And we send that out to probably a quarter of a million people. And I've got another one that does essentially the same thing with over 300,000 names.

INTERVIEWS

If one of your students came to you with a problem, either a personal problem or a business problem they were stressing about, how would you approach helping them feel more at ease or helping them understand what was going on?

I would get them talking about it. They could get into detail if they wanted. I don't let myself get emotionally caught up in the melodrama, but I get them talking. I heard a psychologist by the name of Sharp once say, "People will not share their problem with you until they feel you have the solution to their problem." If they feel you have a solution and you make them feel comfortable, they'll open up. I think they usually answer the problem themselves, if they get talking about it. I'm very good at that and I'm a good listener, and I think that's really the key.

So they start to feel better after you talk to them? Do you do one-on-one discussions?

I don't do a lot of it. I don't have time to do a lot of it any more.

What interests or hobbies do you have other than your business? Is there anything else that fascinates you?

No, I don't have time for anything else. I used to play golf, but I played golf because I thought I should play golf. I was out there one day and I was about halfway through and I said, "I've got to quit. This is aggravating me. I'm not getting enjoyment out of this."

INTERVIEWS

How do you title yourself?
I see myself as a salesman really.

I know we all have to sell things. What would you put under your name as a title?
Author/Speaker.

Not Success Speaker, Personal Development Expert or Motivator?
I think motivation is like a hot shower. You get out of the shower and you're cold really fast. As Napoleon Hill shared … education comes from the Latin word *educo*: to induce, develop or to draw out from within. I think that's what real education does. School has left us on the wrong track. School said read the book, remember what's in the book and if you can repeat it we'll give you a degree. Well there are people with all kinds of degrees, but they don't even know enough to come in out of the rain. I see myself as an educator in the true sense of the word. I really wake people up to their potential. I think when people understand who and what they are, their whole world starts to change.

I like that – wake people up to their true potential. My wife Tosca gives a lot of seminars with regard to nutrition, and she saves up special sayings she knows go over well. Do you have a lot of those?
I've got a zillion of them and they come just when I need them.

INTERVIEWS

How important is personal dress? You always appear, from head to toe, well groomed.

Well if you're doing a seminar, it's very important. People see you long before they hear you, smell you, taste you or touch you. And you're going to leave an impression on their mind just like that. And if it's the wrong one, it may take you half the day to get past it.

At my office we have 12 people in the book department. We put out about 20 titles per year. They're overwhelmed by the thought of trying to monetize. Publishing a book can be a very risky proposition.

The economy is not great. There are a zillion books coming out every year. There's another way. And that's your law of opposites. There's an inside to this house, so there's an outside to it – that's the law of polarity. Price Pritchett put it very well – he said, "The absence of evidence is not the evidence of absence." If there's a way you can't, there has to be a way you can. Well, that's what people fail to understand – they don't understand that they're dealing with laws. They're going by what they see, and they see according to their conditioning. I'll give you a good example. I was conducting a seminar in Chicago not long ago. There was a woman right in the front row. I went over and I said, "If I were to ask the audience, they would say you're black. Is that correct?" She smiled and said, "I guess they would." And I said, "They'd say I'm white." She answered, "Yeah they probably would." Now I said, "My shirt's white, but

I'm not the color of my shirt. If you ever saw a truly 'white' person you'd probably scream and run." And I said, "You're not black. So why do they say you're black and I'm white?" They're saying that because that's what they see. You don't see with your eyes, you see through your eyes – you see with cells of recognition in your brain. Now if you're seeing something that isn't there in this situation, how many other things do you see that aren't there? And the truth is, we see the road blocks – we don't see the openings. We see the walls, but we don't see the doors.

Do you have any regrets about anything that you've done in life?

Absolutely none. I probably used to, but I think I learned a few things along the way. I think I heard it best explained years ago on Johnny Carson one night. Vincent Price was on and George Carlin was sitting in for Johnny Carson. Carlin said, "Vincent, tell us about the new show." And he said, "I think people are going to love it." They had this pilot they were promoting. He said, "It's about a train and I'm the conductor on the train. Now this is a special train. You can buy a ticket and go back to any point in your life that you'd like to start over. And when you get to that point, I'm the conductor, I stop the train and I let you off. I think everybody would like to go back and start over, don't you?" Carlin said, "I don't think so." You could see the executive producers tearing their hair out. He said, "If I went back and changed anything, I wouldn't be me. I like me." And I thought, what a beautiful answer. The show, of course, never made it. I see everything we do as essential to make us who we are, to prepare us to do whatever we're going to do. And I don't think we know what we're going to do. We play with the idea – we think we do, but there's a turn in the road. You're always preparing yourself for something greater. That's why we need the greater awareness.

Tosca was not happy with the way her life was going 10 or 15 years ago. She was dejected, overweight and would pass out in grocery stores from hypoglycemia. She allowed her first husband to mentally and physically control her.
Well, you see that's low self-esteem.

And then when we met, things changed and she's happy with her life. She says she feels like she's just beginning.
Tosca would never want it to happen again, but yet it was necessary to make her who she is. She gained an awareness that the average person doesn't have. I have studied this for 50 years and I am totally convinced that everything that happens, all the crap that goes on in our life, is essential to make us who we are. Think of how much stronger Tosca is today. Let's suppose Tosca came from a nice home and had a nice husband who treated her really nice, and then he died and Tosca moved on. I mean, there'd be no substance and no depth to her.

INTERVIEWS

When she decided to leave her first husband she didn't seek revenge. She merely decided to get successful.

I think she should have sent him love. There's a woman who works with me who's going through a divorce, and she's having a bit of a rough time. And she asked me to tell her something that would help her. I took a piece of paper out of my pocket, and I said, "When you first wake up in the morning, before you do anything, write down 10 things you're grateful for. Then take five minutes and just be really quiet and ask the universe for direction for the day. And send love to all the people who bother you." Now, if you're bothering me and I focus on why you're bothering me, who's in the bad vibration? Hell, you could be out having a great time and I'm in a bad vibration. Resentment is like drinking poison. If I'm sending love, then who has that good vibration? Me. At first it may be very difficult because you don't like them, but you don't have to like them, just send them good energy. And you move into a great vibration.

Do you use a company to get you your speaking engagements or do you do it all through your website?
I don't work through any speaking companies. I've been to the National Speakers Association once, but I found most people went there to try and figure out how to get work. I've always been busy. I get engagements through my website and my contacts.

INTERVIEWS

Did you take public speaking courses?
No, in fact I wouldn't even recommend it. I probably make a thousand mistakes when I'm speaking, but I'll hold your attention all day. Because all I'm talking about is you. If I talk about me, you're not going to be very interested.

Is that the secret of public speaking?
In speaking, always remember it's like broadcasting… you pretend you're talking to only one person. There could be a thousand people there, but you're talking to only one. Everybody else is just listening to you talk to that one person. You really have to want to help them understand what you're saying. And you have to have something of value for them. If you do that, they're going to give you their undivided attention. When a speaker starts to focus on themselves, that's when the audience starts to get bored. They're not interested in you; they're interested in themselves, so if you talk to them about them, they'll give you all day.

I'm not sure how to formulate this question. But when I've got a problem, and it gets into my mind, sometimes it dwells there and it invades my thoughts, stays there and inherits the whole of my mind, and I think about it all the time. I have no solutions and then maybe during the night or when I wake up [snaps his fingers], there's a solution. It's like magic. It's happened two or three times in my life. Can you explain it?

INTERVIEWS

It can happen more often than that. We'll take the mind and divide it into two parts: your conscious mind and your subconscious mind. The subconscious mind is actually universal intelligence. Your subconscious mind is part of everything in the universe. This is also called your emotional mind. If you take the problem and it's an idea you're consciously thinking about, when you go to bed, just ask the universe for the answer. Every question has an answer. Ask for the answer to it. And believe you will get it. Now what you've done is you've taken this and you've turned it over to universal intelligence, your subconscious mind.

The subconscious mind and universal intelligence is the same thing. Sometimes it comes in a dream. When you wake up, instantly ask yourself for the answer. And it may be there, it may not. It sounded like you were doing it unconsciously the way you were explaining it. Well, start to consciously do it. When you're going to sleep just tell universal intelligence: "I want to thank you in advance for the answer to this problem." Give thanks for it. And when you wake up in the morning you'll likely have the answer.

So while you're sleeping, the subconscious mind is looking and grabbing everything it can get?
The mind is always working. The subconscious mind is always here, always moving. The whole universe moves – nothing rests. The law of vibration decrees that everything moves. A body in a coffin is moving. If it wasn't moving

it would never change to dust. There's a great book *The Power of the Subconscious Mind* by Dr. Joseph Murphy. It's a powerful book. It's probably one of the best books on the subconscious mind you'll ever read. As you read his book you'll realize you're dealing with universal intelligence. Everything you've accomplished, that's how you accomplished it. You've built an image in your mind and the image has moved into form.

What does an individual do when he or she has devastating problems like an earthquake destroying everything, or a severely injured son, daughter or spouse? What about a lethal car accident or serious illness, or something else, and we stress over the problem day after day?

Well you have to get rid of that stress. You have to forgive yourself. Forgive means to let it go completely. The problem was absolutely essential or it wouldn't have happened. Why it happened, we don't know. Sometimes you don't know the answer. You have to see everything that happens as good. Nothing is bad. We've got to stop and think and we've got to see the good in things. I had open-heart surgery recently. I had bacteria on the aortic valve and someone asked, "Do you believe you caused that?" I said, "Absolutely, I just don't know what the hell I did." I don't know why I had it. But I do know they virtually killed me: cut me open, dumped ice in my chest to stop my heart. They put me on a heart machine and a lung machine; they collapsed my lungs. They took my heart out, they cut off the aortic valve, they put a pig's valve on there, put it back in, and what amazed me is that it didn't leak! They must've been really good at sewing to hook that in there. I don't know why it happened. But I saw nothing but good in it. I treated the doctors and nurses like they were the most important people in the world and they loved looking after me. I had a wonderful time in Cedars-Sinai Medical Center in LA, the best hospital in the world, and the best doctors.

Is there anything you want to say that I haven't asked you or that you haven't talked about?
No, I think the important thing is that anyone can succeed; they have to believe in themselves and the only way to believe in themselves is to understand more about themselves. I came to a point where I realized I was always trying to figure out belief. I studied the Bible, the Koran, all the religious books. I studied all the psychological books and without exception they all said you have to believe. Our belief system is based upon our evaluation of something. And frequently if we re-evaluate a situation, our belief about it will change. I changed when I started to believe in me. I believed in me because I started to study who I was. I started to understand my body, the relationship of the mind to the body. I started to understand how the mind works. While I was studying, I started to learn more about me and started to believe in me. I have tremendous confidence in myself today because I understand who I

am and how the universe works. It works by law. I don't have to know how to do it. In fact, if I know how to do it I'm probably going sideways. If you know how to reach a goal, you've got the wrong goal. You should be going after something you don't know how to reach. That causes us to stretch and it causes us to pull more out of ourselves. I think the important message is that anyone can win at anything if they really want to – it's all contingent upon belief in yourself.

The book you wrote, *You Were Born Rich* – is that still available?

You can go online and go to bobproctor.com and download it. I've never really been into promoting books. I write programs.

You've got to get into my program. It's 12 DVDs; it's an incredible program. A lady attended a program I was conducting in 2006, Sandy Gallagher, and she was a banking lawyer. She's a very bright gal. She graduated as the number-one banking lawyer in the US 21 years ago. She'd been involved in all kinds of negotiations, and she probably negotiated over $100 billion in deals over the 20 years she was there. Anyway, she came to my seminar and had never heard this information before. She thought if she could get this information into the boardroom, she could do things so much more quickly. So she decided she was going to learn all she could of what I knew. She went through all

INTERVIEWS

our programs. We have a consulting program, and she went through that. And then she made up her mind she wanted to be on the inside of our company. She wanted to build a program – I told her go ahead. She put together a program that a corporate executive would learn from. There are 12 lessons in it; it's really very well done. She produced it, directed it, did the packaging on it – she did the whole thing. And now she's the CEO and president of our company. The program is "Thinking Into Results" and it's available via lscorporate.com.

I appreciate this eye-opening interview, which readers will find most rewarding. Thank you.

INTERVIEWS

Jay Hennick

Jay Hennick is the Founder and CEO of FirstService Corporation, a global diversified leader in real estate services through three platforms: commercial real estate, residential property management and property services. His business, which generates $1.7 billion (USD) in annual revenue, operates in 41 countries around the globe.

The FirstService platforms include Colliers International, the third largest global player in commercial real estate; FirstService Residential Management, the largest manager of residential communities in North America; and TFC, North America's largest provider of property services through franchise and contractor networks. Jay and his wife Barbara contribute to a variety of causes in the area of education and medical research.

RK: Where and when were you born?
JH: I was born in Toronto in 1957.

What did your parents do for a living?
My father ran a jewelry retail store and later a jewelry manufacturing business, and my mother was a homemaker.

INTERVIEWS

As a teenager, you showed your entrepreneurial spirit by founding Superior Pools. Can you describe what this was?

Superior Pools was a company that provided lifeguards and serviced commercial swimming pools for owners of apartments, hotels and condos, schools – all commercial pools. I started the company when I was 16 after working two summers as a lifeguard at an apartment building. I realized there was an opportunity to start a company of my own, servicing swimming pools for apartment building owners and others. As Toronto was growing, developers were adding amenities like swimming pools to help them rent and sell the buildings they developed, and few people had the expertise to manage and service the pools once they were built. There was a law that required the building owner to provide a lifeguard if the building was greater than a certain size, and that created the opportunity I needed. Superior Pools is still very much around today – it is part of a larger division of our company called American Pools. American Pools services more than 2,500 commercial swimming pools and recreation facilities throughout North America and generates about $100 million per annum in revenues.

The money you made from Superior allowed you to further your education and become a lawyer?
Yes.

Did you ever work for others?

Yes. When I went to my parents with the idea of starting my own service company, their reaction, to put it nicely, was that I shouldn't be thinking about being in the pool business as a career opportunity for the rest of my life. They thought I should get a complete education first, become a lawyer or an accountant, or take a business degree. Needless to say, I listened to my parents (as all good children should) and went off to university and became a lawyer. I practiced law for 13 years. I guess I was an employee of the law firm before I became a partner of the firm, but even when I was an employee, I loved every minute of practicing law. At the same time I had recruited a good friend into Superior to help me run it "on the side." Howie Kirshenbaum and Stephen Schecter still run that division of our company to this day.

And then what did you go on to?

When I was practicing law, I spent all of my time with entrepreneurs, business leaders and large corporate clients. I helped them take their companies public, make acquisitions and make dispositions. I got a great understanding for how to handle business issues, legal issues and structural issues. After 13 years of practicing, I decided that I wanted to create a company of my own, and that's how I started FirstService.

How did you get into the real estate business? I

understand you're a global leader in real estate services.

The initial philosophy of FirstService was to be a diversified provider of market-leading service companies. I followed the model of a UK-based service company called Rentokil as well as many US companies in the same area – companies like ServiceMaster, Aramark and American Building Maintenance. All of these companies were highly reputable, incredibly large service-based businesses, primarily people-oriented, with strong brands and low capital expenditures. There wasn't anyone doing this in Canada, and providing services was essentially what I did in the swimming pool business – and what lawyers and other professionals do every day in their own practices. So the initial philosophy of FirstService was to be a diversified service business. As we grew we had five different service lines, all of which we operated in the same way. I found a great mentor in the late Peter Drucker, who you know is very famous, one of the great business advisors of all time. He consulted with Watson from IBM, Sloan from GM and, of course, Jack Welch from GE. I got one of my friends to introduce me and ultimately picked up the phone one day and called Peter and said, "My name is Jay Hennick, I have this business I'm in the process of building and have read most of your books – can we talk?" He was so very helpful. Not only was he prepared to talk, he invited me to his home in Claremont, California, and I carried on a long-term relationship with Peter before he passed away. He helped me develop what is now the FirstService philosophy of operating.

Did you always have confidence that you would be this hugely successful?

I would not really say that. I did have confidence in my abilities to get things done. But ultimately in business it comes down to your personal drive, commitment and your ability to build a team around you. The other quality that cannot be underestimated is judgement. As the business grows, you have to start assembling a team of like-minded people who share your vision and values; people who are as concerned about the business as you are; and people who bring together a variety of skill sets that are complementary to one another. So as I'm sitting here talking to you today, I've got 92 things going on, but I'm still very comfortable that our guys are handling them as well as, or better than, I would be if I were handling them on the front lines. Having a great team is essential to success, especially as the company gets larger.

So you've made a very strong point of finding the best people possible to do the various jobs.

Yes, people who are experts in different areas, and who would complement me. They have to share the same values. With my team, especially the ones around me – each of our divisions operates autonomously, but the ones around me, we know each other so well that just a few words speak volumes about what we are doing and where we have to go. The people who are around the FirstService head office have been around for a long time.

Are they paid employees or do they have extra bonuses and such?
They all have equity in the business and work hard every day to help build our company, so I would say, yes, they have all become wealthy as a result of being involved with a successful company like FirstService.

Can anyone be a success?
Good question. My personal view is that you need to be smart enough – you don't need to be brilliant. The mistake people make is that they think the smartest people become the most successful people. That is simply not true. I was fortunate in that I did pretty well academically; I wasn't top of my class, but I was always in the top 10 to 20 percent. So I don't think you need to be the smartest guy to be successful. Execution is critical, discipline is critical and stick-to-itiveness is critical, but having all of this, together with judgement, makes all the difference in the world.

When problems arise as they do in any business, do you have a specific way of addressing the situation?
In an organization like ours, decision-making happens at various stages of the company, so if it's on the front line,

I'm hoping the driver of that business will make those decisions effectively. But, as it moves up the line, by the time it gets to me, most of the time the decisions that have to be made are new decisions, so there's no precedent to follow. That's where judgement comes in. We have a defined operating philosophy at FirstService. It's on our website: the seven principles of The FirstService Way. We say to our operators, many of whom have equity in the business, "Look, you are great at your business, we have huge confidence in you and we know you will make the right decisions every day. But when it comes to things that are out of the ordinary course, things like an acquisition, a disposition or significant capital expenditure, we need to have the opportunity to talk to you about that in detail, so these are the decisions we want you to make with our input." The bottom line is, with the exception of 16 or 17 things that we need to have input on (many of which are required because we are a public company), you have all the autonomy in the world to run your business as you see fit.

Do you have a business philosophy, something that guides you almost daily?
The seven principles of The FirstService Way! They're on our website, we talk about them all the time.

Did you ever feel like giving up?
If you have a passion for building something unique and different, you never give up. In our case, we have the op-

portunity to build a global leader in real estate services. How many people have that opportunity? When I think of Canadian companies that are truly global, there are a surprising few: Four Seasons Hotels, Fairmont Hotels, Bombardier and Research in Motion. In our case, Colliers International operates in 61 countries around the world. We were founded right here in Canada and we have so many opportunities to grow our business in all parts of the world. I am very excited about what I do. Now, having said all that, there are of course issues that come up every day in our business – issues that are difficult to solve and often trying in personal terms. Just today, we discussed a silly thing that happened in one of our operations, something that could and should have been avoided easily had someone turned their mind to it when it happened. Instead, it was overlooked and the problem grew to the point that it is not so easy to fix. These kinds of things happen all the time. They bother the hell out of you, especially when it costs the company millions of dollars on something that should never have happened in the first place. The key is, you suck it up, fix the problem as quickly as you can and move on. There are no other options.

You undergo stress, but you don't look like you're stressed. So you're beating it. At 54, you look great!
Okay [he laughs]. I hope so. Thanks for the compliment.

What was the turning point in your career when you

INTERVIEWS

realized you were a success, when you said, "Hey, I've really done this!" Was there any specific time?
No, I don't think I'm a success.

I'm astonished that you would say that. So what would it take to make you a success? You're a financial success.
It depends how you measure success. To me, when I look at Isadore (Issy) Sharp from Four Seasons Hotel, he's an 80-year-old man, he's built a fantastic global brand, he was the chairman and CEO of his business and shaped its destiny for more than 50 years – that's successful to me. You look at great entrepreneurs like Frank Stronach – this is a man who has consistently created, created, created through much adversity, overcoming problems, corporate governance issues and he's done it over a long period of time. We've done it for a relatively short period of time, and I hope that when I'm 80 years old and you and I are having another conversation like this and you ask me "Are you successful now?" Maybe then, I might say yes. We have too much work to do to claim to be successful. Also, I think you lose the edge if you start thinking you're successful. If you're not paranoid as hell about everything that goes on, you're done.

Also success is family and kids and personal health....
In that respect I feel very blessed. I have a great wife who

I have been married to for almost 32 years, and three great children. In personal terms, I've had two bouts with cancer that I've overcome; at least I hope I have. I had thyroid cancer when I was around 40 and over the last year, I had a small brain tumor. My face was numb and I've lost my hearing in one ear. It happens, but it's how you deal with it that is critical. There is nothing I can do about any of it other than get the best medical assistance I can, and get on with my great life. I am truly thankful.

Did that keep you out of business for a while?
You know, about a week. I was down for a couple of days and then I picked myself up and said, "You only live once, you have a great family, a great job – how does it help me to be down?" So that's again a measure of drive and determination. Some people have serious health issues and become very depressed, and go into a shell and feel sorry for themselves. In some cases it's a chemical imbalance. I'm not talking about those cases. I am talking about the cases where people just clam up and can't seem to get out of their own way. To those people I say, "Suck it up as best you can and get back into the game." What other options do they have?

I myself was sunbathing in the Bahamas about a year ago and my wife said, "You've got sort of a bald spot on the back of your head, you're getting too much sun." And I joked, "Mad dogs and English-

men lie out in the midday sun." I stayed out and I got a growth there that was skin cancer, and I was shocked. I'd loved the sun all my life and learned my lesson. I know what you're going through, and it's unpleasant. Fortunately, the growth was cut out and I'm fine. Like you I feel fortunate that modern medical methods have helped us beat our illnesses.

And you're reacting in the same way?

Same as you did. It's a nasty thing but...

That's something that has to come out in an interview like this. Everyone has problems – with family, a child, work – all kinds of stuff. There's an old story, I forget who told it but it went something like this: If you were able to package 20 people's personal problems each in their own box and put them in the middle of a room, and then you gave everyone the choice of picking whatever box they wanted, they would select their own. The grass always looks greener – but everyone has issues or problems in their lives.

What do you consider your strengths?
Values, discipline and a passion for what I do – the challenge of doing something great. It's also about treating people well and having them around you to share in the success of your accomplishments.

If a friend came to you asking where he should invest $100,000, how would you advise that person?
It depends. If they have a mortgage, I would pay off your house first. I would take away all personal debt as quickly as you possibly can. That's where you put all of your money. You have a lot more confidence in life if you are debt free. And you shouldn't really be investing until you own your personal assets. I don't know about you, but the day I paid off my mortgage for the first time, I gained a great deal of personal confidence because I always knew I had a house to fall back on if I needed it. Others leverage up to enjoy life, buying stocks and other things, and when the market falls they are in trouble.

If you have no personal debt, then I would say invest in yourself - in a business, in real estate or in something else that you will look after on your own. Other than that, I'm not an investment advisor.

Has any one person been a business mentor to you, from whom you've learned important aspects of business? Was there anyone you looked up to?
There have been a number. My dad first and foremost - being around my dad, listening to him talk about his business, his investments and his business philosophy was a critical part of my development. He helped me gain the

judgement I think I have in business. Also, at a very early age because I'd started my pool business and made some money, we began to invest together. He was my father but also my partner in everything I did. He passed away this year [2011]. I miss him.

Over the years, as our company grew, I also sought out others who had experience with larger companies, including Peter Drucker, and did extensive reading in a number of areas. I relied on good friends and advisors like Peter Cohen, Bernie Ghert, Brendan Calder and others. There are a variety of mentors that I draw upon to help me with particular issues.

What do you do in your spare time – any hobbies?
I have very few hobbies. I work out four or five times a week. I'm up in the morning at 5 a.m. and I do a routine. I think that's sort of part of what I must do. Other than that, I have three kids, so I spend lots of time with them. I've tried every sport known to man, and find most of them boring. I do love to travel with my wife, collect art, build special places to live and enjoy the quieter moments.

Do you have a favorite place to travel to?
I love all of Italy — Lake Como is fantastic and the south is also magical.

It's obvious you go the extra mile in your endeavors.

INTERVIEWS

What stimulated you to first break out from the way most people do things?

I think most people you meet do a lot of talk about doing and they don't do. It's very hard to do; I have never had a problem doing. But others talk; few do.

You're not keen to retire at all?

I could've retired years ago. I have some friends who are selling their businesses and retiring and living what appear to be great lives. I look at it and think *what am I going to do with all that free time?* How many newspapers can I read? How much surfing the net can you do? I have a goal in mind for our company where I'd like to take it; we have a huge canvas for growth — the world; we operate in a huge industry, what more can you ask for? I like the people I work with and I like the scale and diversity of what we do, so I'm not interested in retirement.

Do you feel that being wealthier and more successful than average has increased your level of happiness, or would you have been happy anyway?

I think that having a certain amount of wealth has helped me be happier. I grew up on the other side of the tracks and I knew that a certain amount of wealth would help me get the things I thought would be important in my life. When you get to that point, there's a point of diminishing returns. I may be at that point where you say, "I've got everything I need. Maybe one day I'll buy a place in Florida."

INTERVIEWS

Other than that I've got everything I need; good health, a great wife, great kids, things are just perfect.

Do you want your kids to be in your business?

No. I want them all to go be successful on their own because there's no better feeling in life than being successful in your own chosen line of accomplishment. My kids are all well educated and well traveled, so hopefully they have the tools to find their ways. Maybe one day if they want a partner and I can help them finance something, whatever it is, I will be there for them. But it will be their passion, their challenge, not mine.

Were there any books that helped you in your endeavours?

Tons of books over the years! The first book I read other than what I had to read in school was Dale Carnegie's *How to Win Friends and Influence People.* I reread that book every couple of years, and I insisted my kids read it as well. Self-help or business books written by Norman Vincent Peale, Jim Collins, Colin Powell, Peter Drucker and others have also been helpful.

All of these and others not only help one enhance one's personal effectiveness, they also help in the role as a business leader, branch manager or whatever.

Any regrets about anything?

I regret that my parents aren't around.

INTERVIEWS

How old was your dad?
My dad was 79 when he passed away. My mom was 64 when she passed away from cancer. I miss them both enormously.

Do you accept any public speaking engagements?
Very rarely. I've done it from time to time when someone twisted my arm, but I'm not a guy who seeks the limelight.

What's your website?
firstservice.com

How has FirstService done for investors over the years?
I think pretty well. We have been public for a long time. If you had invested $100,000 15 years ago when we first went public, it would be worth more than $2 million today, so that's a 24 to 25 percent annual return. Our shareholders are happy and when I look at us relative to others we have done pretty well. I'm proud of our accomplishments.

Thank you Jay for an eye-opening interview.

INTERVIEWS

John Cardillo

John Cardillo is a prime example of a self-made man. Not only did he build himself a prize-winning physique, competing internationally in bodybuilding contests with great success, he also forged a chain of 36 fitness clubs, with an annual gross of over $100 million over a period of 30 years. He has a beautiful wife Giselle and two super-active boys, John Jr., 10, and Briden, 8. John divides his time between homes in Ontario, Canada and Miami, Florida.

RK: John, you were born in Italy. At what age did you move to North America? How old are you now?
JC: I was seven years old when my parents came to Niagara Falls on the Canadian-US border. I am 53 years of age.

How would you describe your parents?
They were extremely hard-working, honest people. They had an enormous work ethic, always struggling to work their hardest to pay the basic bills of a simple existence.

What got you interested in going into business for yourself?
As I was growing up in Niagara Falls, I came to understand

that many families in the area were able to support their kids by enrolling them in hockey, soccer and other sports. On March Break they would take off for the Bahamas or even Europe. My parents just could not afford these luxuries. One thing that really got to me was carrying loads of groceries for my mother. Other families had expensive cars whipping past while I was struggling with carrying the heavy bags a considerable distance from the grocery store to our house. Sometimes kids from school would see me traipsing behind my mother and I could sense their reactions. That is when I swore that when I got older I would never find myself without the finer things in life. I wanted like crazy to be successful because these people had their own businesses. I knew then I wanted one day to have my own business.

You are in great shape. When did you first get interested in training?
While still in school I wanted to make the football team so I started lifting weights in the school gym to gain muscle and strength. It worked. I made the team.

What was your first job after leaving school?
I worked part-time in the local gym, helping others to train. I also kept my eyes open and learned how things worked.

And then you opened your own gym in Niagara Falls at age 19?

INTERVIEWS

Everything starts out psychologically, I think, so what happened is the fact that my parents were trying to set up a better life for their kids, and having this immigrant mentality that you are somewhat inferior because you are not part of the melting pot – you're in the worker class as opposed to the business class. Two things kindled my thoughts on working out and on business. One was the fact that working at a simple job wasn't what I believed would lead to the best lifestyle, so I knew I had to be in business. The second was, I remember the first time I went to a sports store and there was a spring set I looked at that had pictures of a bodybuilder using springs to build his body. I looked at the images and thought, 'That's pretty incredible, but is it achievable?' So that had a big impression on me and started the curiosity with working out and whether or not I could build a better physique as the result of training.

I wanted to make the football team, and I decided that working out with weights would be a good avenue, and I started running – all the things that would make me a better athlete. I enjoyed hockey and basketball, but I wasn't tall or big or strong enough. But as I got into weight training, I realized I enjoyed it more than competitive team sports. I loved the feeling of accomplishing new goals with each workout; basically, I was bitten by the iron bug, whereas sports didn't seem to be as important to me as my workouts. After my second year of football in Grade

10, I decided I wanted to go into bodybuilding full time as an objective. That's when I started looking at what bodybuilding could lead to; I changed my whole idea as to my future goals.

At one time I thought I could enjoy becoming a Phys Ed teacher, but I quickly learned that wasn't financially rewarding compared to the potential of owning my own business. So I went to university with the idea of trying to get an education to be better equipped for business. At the same time, as I was competing in bodybuilding and working at a fitness club as an instructor, I started understanding how lucrative and how valuable it was to provide people with the proper instruction and a place to work out. I also realized how few workout clubs there were at the time, so that's where the idea came from. The idea quickly developed to leave school, which I did after the first year, and I was 19 when I opened my first club. My youth and my circumstances in life at the time created two goals: one was business and one was bodybuilding. Business was for the purpose of having a better lifestyle than my parents, and bodybuilding was for my personal satisfaction.

Did everything go smoothly when you first started into the gym business? It seems everyone goes through a period of problems. What kind of setbacks did you encounter as you were building your

empire?

The thing that I regret most in the way I started was that I didn't have enough business education. I had the will-power, I had the work ethic and I was a true entrepreneur. However, I feel that had I continued school and perhaps got an MBA, I would've been better equipped to handle certain challenges in business that a novice encounters – financing clubs, taking the right locations, partnerships, employees – all these things depend on being able to understand business models, being able to understand service models with members. Practical experience is very important, but deeper business wisdom comes from having the education behind you when it comes to leasing, finances, employee relations and developing a strategy that's going to take you further. As you develop it and go along, you're bound to make a lot more mistakes. But I always use mistakes as a lesson that you don't want to pay for twice. You pay for that lesson by making that mistake once and you learn not to repeat it.

Everyone makes mistakes – in a way you feel mistakes are good because you can learn from them. Do you have a business philosophy or something that guides you almost daily?

My business philosophy is that you stick to what you know and you surround yourself with the best possible people that can give you the best advice and the best support for your ideas.

INTERVIEWS

Do you feel that being strong and healthy has contributed to your success in the business world?
Absolutely. The genesis of everything for me has been the knowledge that if I started bench pressing only 100 pounds, those small increments I increased by until I reached 400 pounds were all successes. It took hard work and time. Business is similar to that – the harder you work at making your business work better and improving all aspects of it, the more you're going to be rewarded.

Have you gone into any business activities other than the gym business?
There are parts of my business that involve aspects other than providing people with fitness establishments. We have to provide them with the actual fiscal facility so that they can pay a small monthly fee rather than a large annual payment. I also felt it was important to involve myself in real estate, so I was able to purchase real estate along the way to build clubs that I thought would not only be successful but also in the long run would increase considerably in value.

Did you always know you would be successful?
I always knew that the harder I worked at something, the more I thought about it, the more I planned the best strategy, the better the result would be – maybe someone else

INTERVIEWS

wouldn't stick to it as long as I would. Therefore, I was prepared to invest whatever time and effort was necessary to make it work. From that standpoint, I kept working on something until it provided the result I was looking for.

Can anyone, in your opinion, become a success?
Anyone and everyone can become a success. However, it takes incredible discipline, you have to have a competitive nature, you have to be able to overcome setbacks; you have to really want it, and you can't give up. And it certainly helps if you enjoy what you do.

Has any one person been a business mentor for you, from whom you've learned important aspects of the business?
I like to be a sponge and learn from different people in various fields. I look at and think about their examples of what they've done and how they've succeeded in their fields, and then I wonder how it can be applied to my field. Oftentimes, you can take great examples from all sorts of different companies and different business people that translate into your own business. This has allowed me to implement things I wouldn't have if I'd stuck with the fitness herd.

When issues come up in your business, as they do in every business, how do you tackle them to avoid excessive stress?

INTERVIEWS

I always look at the outcome that I want. It doesn't matter what the problem is, I always question what the outcome is. If the outcome is X, then I try to figure out all the steps required to get to that outcome. Who needs to be deployed or employed to achieve the result I'm looking for?

Go through your typical day, morning to night.
Now my typical day involves a lot of preplanning in the morning. I usually wake up between 4 and 5 a.m. I spend the first two hours planning my day, setting my mind on what is important to do that day – what are the issues, what are the things I want to accomplish. I usually do this between 5 and 7 a.m. because my mind is freshest, I'm not tired and I have peace and quiet because nobody else is up yet in my home. Whether that means looking at documents, making big decisions or planning, I can look at it with clear focus in quiet, having a coffee. That's the time when I really forge what the day is going to be about, and what the future is going to be about. My first two hours of the day are very important to me.

I play with my kids for a bit, they're off to school at 8 a.m., then I make my phone calls unless I have a meeting and need to be at the office. I'm usually at home for about an hour. I leave my home by 9 or 9:30 and get to the office by 10. My first meeting is usually at 11. I don't take lunches or go for lunch meetings whatsoever. I like working straight through the day with meetings and with people in the office. I try to get out to a club or two every week to see what's going on, and I finish off my day by sitting with a couple of key people at my office to review things. I like to have a bit of quiet time at the office at the end of the day between 5 and 8 p.m., looking at financials, decision-making processes. So that's another part of my day that's important.

So there's no doubt that's a long day.
It goes by very quickly – by Friday I'm a bit tired, but I don't feel like I go to work every day. Being in business for yourself is enjoyable, at least for me. If you enjoy what you do then you will never have to work a day in your life.

What are your strengths? What would you say John Cardillo is really good at?
Perseverance and figuring it out. People in business, or in general, are going to be confronted with obstacles. There are two ways to confront them: one is fear, and you back away, and the other is considering the obstacle a challenge and you figure it out. All of the adversity of my life, it affects me, but I try to always take the standpoint during adversity to identify it, figure out how to deal with it, determine the desired outcome and what the best plan is to achieve that outcome.

If someone came to you asking where they could invest $100,000, how would you advise them?

INTERVIEWS

If they had any business savvy, I would review what they were doing and see whether more capital would help them make more money. Or if that wasn't the case, if they were just somebody who had a job and had $100,000 in savings, then I would advise them to find the best money manager with a proven track record, a great reputation, satisfied clients who I'd want to speak to, and I would advise them to put the money with someone who does that for a living and who's very good at it. I would not advise them to go buy a stock or start trading online. That's a fool's way to making money. Paying off any personal debts would be the first requirement.

What is the key factor that's made you successful without which you would not have made it?
In order to be successful at anything, you must love what you do. If you love what you do, naturally you're going to persevere. I sell health and fitness – I don't sell widgets, I don't sell furniture, I don't sell real estate. I try to give my customers the best experienced advice possible because I love the result that fitness and health gives someone. I know the result is so positive that if I can achieve that result with a client or member, then I've done my job and they're going to be a member forever. I really love that aspect of what I do. If I can persevere to give my members the best experience possible, so my business is rewarded by patronage, then I'm achieving what I set out to achieve in the first place.

INTERVIEWS

Do you trust your instincts?

Yes, if every time I said yes but knew I should've said no, had I actually trusted my instinct better, I would've achieved a much better result. So I do trust my instincts.

Thank you, John. I'm sure readers will learn a lot from your entrepreneurial excellence.

INTERVIEWS

Scott Wilson

Dr. Scott Wilson tells us, "There's never been a more exciting time to be in the healthcare industry." Whether you're a healthcare practitioner or an entrepreneur making a living by helping others, the profession is satisfying. As a sole chiropractic practitioner, Dr. Wilson noted that not only did clients come to him with a variety of injuries and ailments, it was clear that clients were in need of additional attention over and above conventional medical care. North Americans face many new health challenges such as diabetes, cardiovascular diseases, obesity, high cholesterol, hypertension, osteoporosis, arthritis and other ailments that are preventable or easily curable through positive lifestyle changes. He found that his patients needed easy access to more resources and treatments, and more personalized attention, care and concern. Serve people well and you, too, will enjoy the rewards.

RK: What did your parents do for a living?
SW: My mother worked as an accounting administrator with the local board of education, and my father was predominantly in a sales position.

Are you married, with any children?
I'm currently not married, though I have two children: Olivia, who's nine, and Nicole, who's two.

INTERVIEWS

How old were you when you first became self-employed?

Throughout university, I worked in jobs that were very heavy in commission. My jobs always had upsides to them. But after graduating as a chiropractor in 1994, every role I took was on a percentage up until I bought into my first clinic a year later in 1995. I graduated 17 years ago, and I've never received a salary along the way.

What was your first venture?

In May of 1994, I graduated as a Doctor of Chiropractic from the Canadian Memorial Chiropractic College. I went to McGill University, and I was accepted into chiropractic at a very young age. I was 20 years old when I was accepted after two years at McGill and graduated at 24 as a doctor. I proceeded to perform locums for doctors, which involved taking over when they were on vacation. I always wanted to learn how different practices ran. I made a formal agreement with John Cardillo of Premier Fitness clubs in 1995 to open a clinic in one of his gyms. In four-and-a-half months I ended up buying out my partner's shares, and subsequently started on my own with this practice. After two months, the clinic was so busy that I was spending up to 16 hours a day treating patients in a variety of ways, often from 7 a.m. to 11 p.m. Upon realizing my success – and this was about a 400 square-foot place, very small and the lease I had was a base plus percentage to the landlord – I offered Cardillo $24,000 up front. I think he thought I had marbles in my head to prepay a rent, but at this point I knew I was going to be a success.

Consequently, I came up with several new and effective patient-management protocols, offered different packages for patients and developed ways of being able to integrate products into the chiropractic treatments, and all of these treatments were passive. They were all hands-on treatments done by myself. Over the next four years, I kept bringing in new chiropractic graduates who were doing internships so I could teach them how to run a practice. Only after my accountant pointed out the enormity of my billings did I realize these were two to three times greater than most other chiropractors running similar-sized practices. In 400 square feet at the age of 27, I was doing okay.

By then, Cardillo saw what I was doing and wanted me to open up in other locations. Because I had these young chiropractic grads working with me, it was very easy for me to place people inside other locations. I had six clinics by the year 2000. I then started learning about the rehabilitation business, which is an active treatment model – active meaning exercise. What's curious is that I'd spent nearly six years practicing in a health club but never once gave any of my patients exercise-based therapy. It was all passively based. I learned about rehabilitation, especially from the motor-vehicle-accident perspective, and then proceeded to bring physiotherapists into my business. Not only did it increase revenue, but it also gave patients more value and provided them with a better solution to most of their conditions. From 2001 to 2006, I worked on bringing in these physiotherapists, kinesiologists and chiropodists into the chiropractic model and expanded to 17 clinics.

In 2004, I realized that expansion without owner operators made it very difficult for success in *every* location. I was frustrated that salaried doctors were not taking their practices as seriously as I did when I was an owner operator. Consequently, I merged a few, reducing it to 12, put partners in every one, incentivized them by having them invest in the clinic and introduced a profit-sharing model, which completely turned around my business.

How did your profit-sharing model work?
I created a formula based on cash-flow profit versus accrual profit: the deposits minus the withdrawals on any given month. I gave all my new partners the opportunity to have no ceiling on what they were able to make, which injected a new entrepreneurial spirit in their attitudes, resulting in a greater success of the clinic. Along with the entrepreneurial lessons, I provided leadership by writing manuals and formalizing the operational protocols of the clinics. From August 2005 until about 2008, our business skyrocketed. I built up a corporate marketing group, relationships with medical doctors, plus I built up a positive relationship with the health-club industry.

INTERVIEWS

Now Scott – word is that your patients love you. Why would that be?

I truly care not only about the condition within the patient, but the patient with the condition. So when I looked at patients, I didn't look at the condition they came in with. I look at it more from the standpoint that this person is coming to me as a trusted healthcare provider so I need to give them solutions that go beyond the norm. It was very common for me to take someone's physical ailment and put it into a dossier with many other health-related aspects they should be focusing on and for their benefit, referring each patient to other medical professionals. I'm a firm believer in taking a patient and educating that individual to better understand his or her condition. When patients are educated enough to see the value, they'll care more and they'll respect me more. The relationship I had with my patients was based on education, and the more I could educate them beyond why they came in, the better.

Would it be fair to say that you take over where a medical doctor might not have the capacity or inclination to follow through all the time?

Yes, I mean, not to be political but healthcare currently is to my mind unsatisfactory. Patients seek treatments for maladies. I think the important thing is to recognize that every person can be better than they are today. Someone has to lead the way. We have to give more value all the way through, so a patient knows that Dr. Wilson of Physiomed is truly their trusted healthcare partner, beyond just the conditions they have, taking loads off the medical profession. We now have to be able to step up and provide the type of service that patients really want, but don't know where to find. And that's what we do.

Do you have a specific way of treating each patient, or do you draw from, say, acupuncture to naturopathy, massage or remedial exercise, or whatever, to offer a variety and tailor treatments to individual patients?

Absolutely. The term I want to own is interdisciplinary. While we've heard of multidisciplinary, which means go to some place – a center, a hospital, a clinic – and there are multiple disciplines available, interdisciplinary would involve these particular disciplines, whether physio, chiropractic, acupuncture, naturopathy, exercise training or massage therapy, looking at metabolic conditions in blood, osteoarthritic conditions, or neuromusculoskeletal strains and sprains, looking at all of these entities but also getting a community of education between all of the involved parties. That way, the patient is at the center of the nexus of all of these disciplines, and then all of these disciplines can work in an environment where they're helping each other. We at Physiomed have really prided ourselves on ensuring that there's an interdisciplinary communication. It's my experience that patients not only respond better but they become more educated, they see more value and refer their friends through word of mouth. All good stuff.

When problems arise, as appears to be inevitable, do you have a specific way of tackling the situation?
Yes; the most important thing is experience, so the first thing I will do with any problem is see if I can on some level relate it to a situation I've dealt with before. I immediately look at how I dealt with that previous situation and figure out where the similarities lie. I'm very good at being black and white, and not emotional. I look at the facts to make decisions. Those who know me would say that I'm very pragmatic and believe in being totally fair. I'm a big believer in the asset of people, so when it comes to the solutions, I very rarely look for a quick, fast solution in anything. I look at where a problem is and try to see a solution in time, concerning the people who are involved. I tend to see the good in people. If they've messed up or if a situation arises, I think in most cases they want to be part of the solution, even if it means there's short-term pain, they'll be part of the long-term gain. I tend to look at the opportunity, and it's served me well.

You have a very unique approach to the business – you do things in a different way to the norm. Did you have to think long and hard to develop your strategy or way of doing business or did it come to you naturally?

INTERVIEWS

I believe that the greatest value I offer my Physiomed partners and franchisees is to teach them how to run the best patient-care clinics to be found anywhere. In turn, this ensures that they are successful, and ultimately contribute to my success. My attitude has always been that I may be at the top of the ladder, but I can't get to my success without making people successful below me. It is always in my mind to make sure that my partners do well, so that I, too, will enjoy success. Their success will translate to mine. If you do that, you don't get into a lot of middle management. People trust me, are loyal to me, and they know that I truly want their success. Every person I've worked with and every partner I have is not only with me, they want to continue to grow with me. I think that's everything – making sure their success ties into my success.

When did you first get the idea that you were a success? Because you obviously are….
I was always a good student; very intense. I was always captain of the team, so I knew I could be a leader. I think 1996 was my real turning point toward success. I had taken over this clinic from my partner and I really didn't know what I was doing. I had student debt up to my eyeballs, I'd just given my landlord a year's worth of rent up front. It was January, and there's always a lull of patients after Christmas, so this was January 1996, and I was walking and thinking, "What the heck? What am I going to do?" I sat down and started thinking about how I could continue to give value

to patients, but I had to start thinking about the financial aspects of how I would make my clinics more successful than others. That's when I got creative, expanded my services, offered packages and so forth. Within two months, business had increased so substantially that I knew I had a gift, that I had an ability to be influential, which ties into one of my two main mentors at a high level, Dale Carnegie. The other is Napoleon Hill. I knew I could influence people and I knew people wanted to be around me – I felt that from my patients.

Other than John Cardillo, Napoleon Hill and Dale Carnegie, has anyone been a business mentor to you?
Bob Proctor put me onto Napoleon Hill and that helped me get to the idea of opening more clinics. I have some mentors, but basically I learn from everyone. I try to see that everyone has a specialty role in what they do and therefore I've been able to learn accounting by being very close to my accounting team, learn financing by being close to the bank. At every level, I've been someone who's been pretty much a study of any doctrine that comes around me at a high level. John and Bob really helped, and Dale Carnegie's *How to Win Friends and Influence People* has been a bible of mine for quite some time.

I bet you were top of your class at school and college, right?

Yes, I was always near the top of my class. Even when I wasn't prepared, I had the confidence to be able to do well, even if I wrote a completely different exam I had the confidence to be able to get the mark. I always knew that I could meet with anybody, sit down with them and sway them to understand where I was coming from and what I wanted to do.

Can anyone, in your opinion, be a success?
I think success is really an ability to hit goals. So can anybody successfully hit the goals they set for themselves? Yes. To be an ultra-successful person, I like to keep score. However, I keep score against myself and not against anyone else. I think that in order to be a high-level successful person, you have to have extreme intensity, discipline, and you have to have a competitive nature. Some like to compete against others. I find you really have to compete against yourself to continually raise the bar. And I think the most important thing that would make it really difficult for people to achieve highest success is the fact that you have to know how to reinvent yourself. You have to know how to evolve. You have to not do any wholesale changes but take the core of what you've been doing and always know you can make it a little better. If you're afraid of change or you think that you are at the pinnacle of your business, you'll never be at the highest level of success.

I've often noticed that when you do something well,

nothing much happens. When you do it very well, a little something will happen. But when you do it in an absolutely excellent manner with utmost passion, things will snowball with success. What are your thoughts on this?

I always tell people that luck is created, not found. Opportunity comes to those who attract. People want to be led by leaders, and people want to be around people who are leaders. When someone can feel that you do things extremely well, that you're at the top of your game, that you're someone who is influential and respected, they want to be with you. And it's funny; it's not always direct. Even people who aren't necessarily in your business want to be associated with you. I find that I have more opportunities than I could ever imagine. I have to push them back because people get around you, and without sounding too existential it's like an aura. There's an aura you give off if you're someone who's been ultra successful, someone who is confident. That's the other trait – you need to have confidence. If you don't have ultra confidence, where you can feel like that, then you're going to come up short.

I guess you pay some of your staff a salary, but most of them have a vested interest in the business, which you're happy to give them. Right?

Everyone used to ask me, "What is your end game? What do you want to do?" And I couldn't answer because as a striving entrepreneur, you never want to think there's a zenith and there's an end. To me it was always, "Well, who knows? I'm happy and I'm just going to continue to grow and grow and grow." I want people who truly have a piece of the action. So franchising was the way I went. The franchise model absolutely ties in perfectly with the way I run my businesses, which is like an owner-operator. I think as long as your model is strong and people see the successes of others working with you, they want to be a part of that.

Were there any books aside from *Think and Grow Rich* and *How to Win Friends and Influence People* that you think were very helpful to your business?
John Maxwell's *The 21 Irrefutable Laws of Leadership* was a great book. I recommend it only because leadership is so important at whatever level you're at. But there are certain things you need to carve in stone to be a leader, so I found that book helped me, along with those other two. I never really got into a lot of the books – I really stuck to my doctrine of Dale and Napoleon. I saw Dale Carnegie with the qualitative book, or the book on how to deal with people to make them feel important, to make them feel like they were more important than anything else. And then Napoleon Hill taught me that by teaching my partners how to be successful, I, too, will benefit financially.

Did you ever feel like giving up during any of this time?

I think because I am a doctor by profession, there was always the fact that whatever challenges might arise, I could go back to my roots and treat patients – which I do, by the way, once a week. Knowing that was always there (it's kind of an odd consolation prize, saying I could go back and do what many people went to school for years to do, and be a success at it), I would never quit. Don't put yourself in a position where you can't use time to help remedy a situation. Fortunately, I've never put myself in a situation where I've had to make quick, fast moves in my business so I've never felt the stress to have to give up anything. I have learned to be patient. When I hit a wall, I can slowly gear down, make a change and then ramp back up again. I'm passionate for healthcare, and I feel strongly about helping to deal with the challenges and healthcare crisis within our governments. Our population's not getting healthier. Go to any city and look at the buildings; you're going to see a bank, an insurance company or a government building. As long as you can understand those institutions exist, and you're in a business that's supported by banks and insurance companies and the government, how can you go wrong? I'm happy to contribute to help society by educating people on better health practices.

What are your plans for the future?
I want to continue to build out the Physiomed brand across Canada, North America and ultimately worldwide.

By that, I mean educating people to take control of their health and provide a center or clinic that allows them to do that. I want to put value back into people's health again. That being said ... a quick little sidebar – because of the Internet, today's patients are far more educated than they were when I practiced, so I've recognized that the role of Physiomed and health practitioners isn't so much to regurgitate diagnoses – patients can read about their conditions online. It's to give solutions and to go beyond why the patient came in. I want to continue what I enjoy, contribute to my partners' and franchisees' success, make positive contributions toward people's health and ultimately create a company that has a stellar reputation for providing quality healthcare.

What is your website?
physiomed.ca

INTERVIEWS

Richard Cooper

Richard Cooper is the quintessential entrepreneur. His main business is Cardinal Couriers, a company that has built its reputation as the most reliable pre-8 a.m. delivery service for time-sensitive goods and parts.

Richard played a big part in helping the paintball industry become more sophisticated. He and his brother developed a repeating gun to fire paintballs, and then they developed a water-soluble paintball that was the precursor of what we have today.

Richard has a beautiful wife Marilyn, and they share a blended family of five children. He has a huge interest in personal fitness and in flying, the latter taking much of his organizational skills in planning air shows throughout North America.

RK: Richard, you're a hugely successful business-man with a passion for flying. How did your interest in aircraft and flying develop?
RC: As a young child, I always wanted to fly. And I'm not sure why – initially I wanted to fly helicopters, so I checked into it in 1972 and it was way too expensive. It was $10,000 to get a licence. So I got a private pilot's licence and just

kept on progressing from there until I eventually learned to fly a helicopter in 1986.

What was your first job coming out of school?
I started working at Litton Systems to build guidance systems. Prior to GPS, these systems were used to allow aircraft to determine where they were and where they needed to go.

You wanted to be a commercial pilot, but your eyesight was not up to scratch for that. Is that true?
Yes, I actually wanted to be a military fighter pilot, but the military wouldn't take me because I wore glasses. Then I wanted to be a commercial pilot, but the airlines back then had the same idea – if you wore glasses they weren't interested. That's all changed now, but back then you had to have perfect vision without glasses.

So in those days you had the energy and ambition to be a fighter pilot. That shows some enthusiasm beyond the norm, that's for sure. What was your first business when you decided to go out on your own as an entrepreneur?
It was all done out of home, small projects for other companies. At one point my brother, father and I made guitar cords, we made luggage racks for Corvettes, we did small electronic amplifiers.

INTERVIEWS

Unbelievable. What was next?

We just kept working away at it. We started all at the same time. My dad was a tool and die maker, I was into electronics and my brother was into sales, so we just pooled those three talents to cover all aspects of the business and we kept working at it over the years, making money and putting it back into the business.

What other businesses did you go into apart from that?

My brother and I, we basically changed the paintball industry from what it used to be to what it is today. Originally the game started long ago as capture the flag – we played it as Cubs (Cub Scouts). Then as we got older we used to play it with BB guns, which wasn't too good. Eventually the game was played with a Nelspot marker, which was used by cattlemen and forestry agents to mark cows and trees. It was a single-shot gun that fired oil-based paint. My brother and I developed a repeating gun to fire the paintball, and then developed a water-soluble paintball, which is fundamentally what the game is today.

So you really reengineered paintball?

Yes, my brother and I did it in the basement of our house.

Are you still involved in that in any way?

No, we got out of that business in the late '70s.

INTERVIEWS

Did it make you any money, or what?

Oh yes, we did very well with it. We've been pretty successful in a lot of different ventures – not that everything's been successful – but we try something and if it doesn't work, we try something else. Paintball did well for us.

That reminds me of a meeting you and I had yesterday with Mr. Arnold Schwarzenegger, former Governor of California, who said a similar thing: "Don't be frightened to fail because it's a learning experience and you just move on."

That's true. I had a conversation with my oldest stepdaughter a while back. She was having a hard time in school, and was getting a bit down about it. She was feeling pretty low, and I said to her, "You know there's no disgrace in failing, but there is in not trying. You just have to keep trying something. Sometimes you have to do it a different way in order to get to the top, sometimes you have to step back and take a different route."

Do you have a business philosophy? In other words, what advice would you give a person focusing on or starting out in business?

I'm very strong in honesty and integrity. I believe over a period of time that those traits may slow you down in different instances, but over the long period of time they're going to win out. Truth and honesty will always prevail.

INTERVIEWS

In your opinion, can anybody be successful?
Anybody *can* be successful. I came from a typical lower-middle-class family. We weren't involved in business; I didn't have any background in business. My formal business training was Grade 9 business. From there on I did electronics, but I always believed in treating people fairly. I like to treat people the way I'd like to be treated. It will come back to you.

Today, what would a typical day's work look like?
I like to get up in the morning and work out first thing. I spend mornings in the office, and then in the afternoons I try and do appointments and stuff like that. I get home in decent time so I can get in another workout before dinner.

You have a courier company, right?
Cardinal Couriers Ltd. – it's a land-based courier service.

How many staff would be involved in running that?
There are presently just fewer than 300 employees.

What do you consider your strengths?
My biggest strength would be that I'm a good judge of people and a good judge of character. I'm also a people person, so I believe very strongly in people. I remember recently there was a kind note, an article written by a former employee titled "Fond Memories of Mr. Cooper," and he commented on how much he enjoyed working with me. I

think that's a very important aspect of business. Some people like to manage through intimidation; I like to manage through respect. I think people work much harder when they respect you than when they're fearful of you.

What would you consider your weakness(es)?
Well that's probably also my weakness. Because of the nature, I always give people the benefit of the doubt; I'm very trusting and that's come back to bite me in the butt a few times. But, I said a long time ago that I refused to allow other people to change the way I am, so I still give people the benefit of the doubt. I try to be very careful, but at the end of the day I still believe in the honesty and integrity of people.

Have you had any real downturns in business that got you worried, where things fell apart, that upset you at the time?
Many times. My brother and I have had more than a dozen different businesses, and we've had our ups and downs. I've gone through several recessions, including this last one which was the worst one, being 2009 and 2011. I sort of relate to Winston Churchill when he said: "If you're going through hell, just keep on going." That's right, too – you just don't stop. You just keep pushing forward.

INTERVIEWS

Even though you may have felt like giving up, you never gave up?

That's another quote from Winston Churchill: "Never, never, never, never give up." I believe that 100 percent. I mean, if you give up you're going to fail because you've given up. If you keep trying, it's not a guarantee of success, but it's a guarantee that you're going to have a possibility of success. That's what I think you have to strive toward, and that's what I think about all the time. I'm always thinking positive, positive, positive. I get up in the morning and sometimes feel a lot of weight on my shoulders, but that leaves my mind very quickly within seconds because every single morning I get up out of bed thinking, 'Wow, what a great day. I woke up. That's a start to a great day. The first day I don't wake up, that's the start of a bad day.' And I haven't had one of those yet. (Laughter.)

You're above ground. Let's enjoy it.

That's right. Every day is a great day because no matter how bad your problems are, someone else's are worse. I just look at all the situations, I think about all the positive aspects I have in my life, I consider myself to be blessed and I just keep moving forward.

Looking back on your business career, was there a turning point when you went from struggling a little bit to where you thought, 'Wow, I'm really making it now – I've really made it.'

It wasn't so much one business, but it was a period of time. After working for eight years, we never took any money out of the company. We just kept putting the money back in. After about eight years, at that point we had started to finally gain some ground. We were selling a system that I designed over 30 years ago, a backup system, which we still sell today, mostly in the US. Canadians seem a little more reluctant at trying things, but that's been a contingent success for us through the years.

Tell me about your father and his influence on you in the early days.
My father taught me a lot of good things. He was a very quiet sort of fellow. I remember when he passed away, his friends would come up to me and tell me that my father never had a bad thing to say about anybody. I can remember growing up, a couple of things that really stand out. He told me that if anyone was paying you to do a job, you should do the best job you possibly can, because that's the job they deserve to get from you. He also taught me that I should do a job right the *first* time. Take the time, do it right. He couldn't figure out how people could never find the time to do a job properly the first time but they could always find the time to get it right the second time. I've always carried both of those thoughts in my mind throughout my career. It has made a big difference because it's a good way to look at things.

INTERVIEWS

So he was teaching you to give your very best that you could on any job that you undertook.

All the time.

Give people what they want and they'll give you what you want.

Exactly. I remember one of my early jobs pumping gas. It was in a relatively short period of time, the guy put me in charge and made me a manager, because I was so enthusiastic. I basically have enjoyed every single job I have ever done, and I have done some pretty lowly jobs, but I don't look at them as being "Oh, I'm pumping gas." You know, I'd be out there in the rain sometimes pumping gas, but I was happy. Why? Because I had a job. I was working and I was excited. I've never ever had a job I didn't learn something from.

Has there been anyone else who's influenced you in a strong way, other than your father?

Not specifically. I've always paid attention to anyone who spoke positively. I'm very driven by people who are passionate. It doesn't matter what you are passionate about, but you have to be passionate about something. And when you're passionate about something, you're going to be successful. Why? Because passion is what drives you. Over the years, through great effort comes great success. If you're passionate and driven, you're going to get there. It may take you a little while and you might run into problems.

But, you know what, if it was really easy, everybody would do it. It's not easy, but at the end of the day it's worth it. And not only that, but your sense of satisfaction is an important part of your positive outlook on life. Remain positive at all times, think positively, move positively. I've always told my sons to stand tall and walk proud. When you're going somewhere, go there with conviction, go there with a purpose. You want to personify confidence and the ability to do what you're going to do, and then you'll be successful.

Do you trust your instincts or do you rely on business data?

I trust a lot in my instincts. I look at data as much as I possibly can, but I trust my instincts, too, and they've done me well over the years. Your instincts become even more valuable as you grow older.

What interests do you have other than business and flying?

I've got a few different hobbies. I'm an amateur radio operator, I am a scuba diver. I weight train. I'm interested in reading, I read a lot. Flying takes up a lot of my life – I'm extremely passionate about it. I find it challenging, and that's one of the reasons I get so excited about it.

You actually own an eight-seat helicopter in addition to an L-29 Viper and a MiG-15. Am I right that there are only about six of these Russian MiG-15s

still existing in the world?

There are probably only about six that are still flying. There were more of that aircraft than any other ever produced. Numbers vary as to how many were completely built. But this was a cold-air war fighter that was first introduced over the skies of Korea in 1950, scaring everybody to death on our side of the fence because they had no idea the Russians had built this. Throughout the Communist Bloc countries somewhere between 15,000 and 18,000 were built. Only a handful of them are really still flying.

You are known as being very generous to your friends and employees and taking them up in your helicopter on occasion. Did you not reward your employees at one Christmastime in this way?

For several years we've brought the helicopter into the company to take employees on rides. We still do a lot of charity work. Recently there was a baby Kaylee (Vitelli), a baby girl at Sick Kids Hospital that needed to get home, and they were looking for a helicopter. We picked her up and flew her home. We still do a lot of stuff like that. And we enjoy it.

How old are you, Richard?

I'm 57.

You have a lot of information to offer and you're very inspiring with your beliefs on how to live life.

Well, I've been very, very blessed in my life. I am fortunate enough that I'm in my own business and it allows me to do other things. One of the things I do is motivational speaking at high schools, talking about attributes of either a high school education or a college education, how much you can do with just a limited amount of education, showing students they really can succeed and excel. I talk about positive thinking and how to be successful, how to get ahead.

I tell people all the time to never give up, always think positively, try, try, try. If it doesn't work, try something else. I've always found there are many different ways to get to the end result. Sometimes it takes a while, but eventually you're going to find a better way to do something.

Don't get dejected by failure.
Right, and people say that all the great inventions have already been done; that's not true. Just recently, within the last two years, we got a patent issued on a device we designed and built for a courier company, and then we realized other companies would be interested in this product. So there are always new ideas out there. Usually, necessity is the mother of invention because something comes up. Keep your eyes open. I always figure, you can't learn anything when your mouth is in gear, but you sure can when your ears are open. That's important!

NOTES

ACKNOWLEDGMENTS

My wife Tosca Reno has to be the first on my list of people to whom I owe a great big "Thank you!" You were the one doing the cooking, dishes and the bed making while I was at the kitchen table merely formulating words, sentences and paragraphs. And it isn't the matter of balancing workloads. You also were ensconced in the writing of your own book, *Your Best Body Now* (Harlequin). I owe you big time.

To my parents, no longer with us... wow! Mom, you gave me so much confidence that I could do well in life if I applied myself, and your daily display of love made me feel important. And Dad, your strictness frightened me at times, but you taught me discipline and to "never be a letdown" to anybody. Your display of love and affection for your only son came late, but it did come during that last decade. Thank you.

And Gino. Whom I have known since you were 15 at art school in the gentle town of Norwich in the UK. We have had conversations for almost 60 years. At least half of what I know has come from you. All hugely accepted and grateful for. You were always there in times of sadness or difficulty. Thank you.

To our four girls, Chelsea, Kelsey-Lynn, Kiersten and Rachel, who give life and drama to our house. To my mother in-law Tina for her bright-eyed passion for life, and zest for conversation. Thank you, ladies.

To John and Giselle for their friendship and advice, to Rich and Marilyn for their kindness, and to Tony and Joanie for their humor. You guys are greatly appreciated.

I owe a debt of gratitude for my editors Wendy Morley, Amy Land, Meredith Barrett and Brittany Seki at RK Pubs, for making sure my sentences make sense, and to Sarah Wells for her nimble-fingered computer work.

I am thrilled to have America's undisputed best book designer, Gabby Caruso, take charge of making *Bull's Eye* the quality product it is. Thank you Gabby.

My thanks to Jessica Hearn and Brian Ross for an exemplary design for *Bull's Eye*. Their work is beyond excellent and I am thankful for both of them.

Chris Barnes lends good sense and a keen eye to web design, and Jeannie Mahoney helps keep everything running smoothly. My thanks to both of you.

And to you Bob Proctor. I blush at the words of your foreword for this book. Way, way too generous.

And to the long since departed Napoleon Hill. You started this whole "personal achievement" thing with your blockbuster *Think and Grow Rich,* the landmark bestseller that taught us all the secrets of success. We are indebted beyond belief.

And finally to Braden, my dearest love, whose chronic head injury from an automobile accident kept you without voice or mobility. I am forever indebted for conveying the true meaning of courage. I love you Braden.

RECOMMENDED READING

Here are some of my favorite personal development books. If possible, I suggest you check out as many of them as you can. I've also included a few recommendations from my friends.

Byrne, Rhonda, *The Secret.* Atria Books/Beyond Words, 2006.

Canfield, Jack, *The Success Principles: How to Get from Where You Are to Where You Want to Be.* HarperCollins Publishers, 2004.

Carlson, Richard, *Don't Sweat the Small Stuff About Money: Spiritual and Practical Ways to Create Abundance and More Fun in Your Life.* Hyperion, 2000.

Carnegie, Dale, *How to Win Friends and Influence People.* Simon and Schuster, 1936.*^•

Clark, Glenn, *The Man Who Tapped the Secrets of the Universe.* The University of Science and Philosophy, 1989.

Colvin, Geoff, *Talent is Overrated: What Really Separates World-Class Performers from Everybody Else.* Portfolio Trade, 2010.+

Covey, Stephen R., *The 7 Habits of Highly Effective People.* Free Press, 2004.

Dyer, Wayne W., *Excuses Begone!* Hay House, 2011.

Hill, Napoleon, *The Law of Success.* Tarcher/Penguin, 2008.

Hill, Napoleon, *Think and Grow Rich.* Combined Registry Company, 1937.*•

Kohe, Martin J., *Your Greatest Power.* Napoleon Hill Foundation, 2005.+

LaLanne, Jack, *Live Young Forever: 12 Steps to Optimum Health, Fitness and Longevity.* Robert Kennedy Publishing, 2009.

Lindsell-Roberts, Sheryl, *Speaking Your Way to Success.* Houghton Mifflin Harcourt, 2010.

Maxwell, John C., *How Successful People Think: Change Your Thinking, Change Your Life.* Center Street Publishing, 2009.•

Murphy, Dr. Joseph, *The Power of Your Subconscious Mind.* Wilder Publications, 2008.+

Pritchett, Price, *You2: A High-Velocity Formula for Multiplying Your Effectiveness in Quantum Leaps.* Pritchett and Associates, 1994.+

Proctor, Bob, *You Were Born Rich.* Life Success Pacific Rim, 2003.

Reno, Tosca, *The Eat-Clean Diet® series.* Robert Kennedy Publishing, eatcleandiet.com.

Reno, Tosca, *Your Best Body Now: Look and Feel Fabulous at Any Age the Eat-Clean Way.* Harlequin Books, 2010.

Robbins, Anthony, *Awaken the Giant Within: How to Take Immediate Control of Your Mental, Emotional, Physical and Financial Destiny!* Free Press, 1992.

Rohn, Jim, *7 Strategies for Wealth & Happiness: Power Ideas from America's Foremost Business Philosopher.* Three Rivers Press, 1996.

Sapolsky, Robert M., *Why Zebras Don't Get Ulcers.* Holt Paperbacks, 2004.

Sayre, Kent, *Unstoppable Confidence: How to Use the Power of NLP to Be More Dynamic and Successful.* McGraw-Hill, 2008.

Templar, Richard, *Rules of Wealth.* Pearson Prentice Hall, 2007.

Templar, Richard, *The Rules of Work: The Unspoken Truth About Getting Ahead in Business.* Prentice Hall, 2005.

Thomas, Peter H., *Be Great: The Five Foundations of an Extraordinary Life.* Franklin Green Publishing, 2010.

Trump, Donald J., *Think Like a Champion: An Informal Education in Business and Life.* Vanguard Press, 2010.

Vitale, Joe, *The Attractor Factor: 5 Easy Steps for Creating Wealth (or Anything Else) From the Inside Out.* Wiley, 2008.

Walton, Sam, *Sam Walton: Made in America.* Bantam Books, 1993.

Welch, Jack, *Winning.* HarperCollins, 2005.

Winget, Larry, *You're Broke Because You Want to Be: How to Stop Getting By and Start Getting Ahead.* Gotham Books, 2008.

Zelinski, Ernie J., *Career Success Without a Real Job: The Career Book for People Too Smart to Work in Corporations.* Visions International Publishing, 2009.

Ziglar, Zig, *Better than Good: Creating a Life You Can't Wait to Live.* Thomas Nelson, 2007.

* Especially recommended by Robert Kennedy

+ Recommended by Bob Proctor

^ Recommended by Jay Hennick

• Recommended by Scott Wilson

BIOGRAPHY

Robert Kennedy spent his formative years as a lover of both art and bodybuilding, often combining the two passions as a writer and illustrator for many popular muscle magazines. Bob was also a high school art teacher, but at heart he has always been an entrepreneur. In the late 1960s he began creating and selling mail-order bodybuilding courses, and he used that experience and the finances acquired to start his own magazine, *MuscleMag International*, put together on his kitchen table in 1974.

Like any successful person, Bob could be audacious. He printed 110,000 copies of his first issue ... and then tried to sell it! Sell it he did, and a publishing powerhouse was born. Robert Kennedy Publishing now produces five magazines: *MuscleMag International*, *Oxygen*, *Reps!*, *American Curves* and *Clean Eating*, in addition to many special issues. In recent years Bob has added books to his roster, and has seen many hits such as *The Eat-Clean Diet*® series.

But Bob's success comes not only from his business. He lives life with a passion and wants to help others learn to do the same. He is an accomplished and respected artist and has come back from personal tragedy to have a wonderful marriage and family life few could rival. Recently Bob received the Lifetime Achievement Award from Arnold Schwarzenegger for making notable contributions to the fitness industry and offering a lifetime of service to the enhancement of sports performance and promotion. Bob lives north of Toronto.